DAISY CAKES BAKES

DAISY CAKES BAKES

KEEPSAKE RECIPES
— *for* —
SOUTHERN LAYER CAKES, PIES, COOKIES,
and more

KIM NELSON

Clarkson Potter/Publishers
NEW YORK

Published in the United States by Clarkson Potter/
Publishers, an imprint of the Crown Publishing
Group, a division of Penguin Random House LLC,
New York.
crownpublishing.com
clarksonpotter.com

CLARKSON POTTER is a trademark and POTTER
with colophon is a registered trademark of
Penguin Random House LLC.

Library of Congress Cataloging-in-Publication Data
is available upon request.

ISBN 978-0-451-49941-7
Ebook ISBN 978-0-451-49942-4

Printed in China

Book design by Sonia Persad
Cover design by Mia Johnson and Sonia Persad
Cover photography by Kristin Teig

10 9 8 7 6 5 4 3 2 1

First Edition

This book is dedicated to my biggest fans:
Mama and Daddy, I love you!

CONTENTS

INTRODUCTION

I grew up catching lightning bugs, playing in the creek, and making mud pies. I went barefoot more than I wore shoes, including while walking in the chicken pen to gather eggs with my grandmothers and great-aunt. We took those eggs in the house and put them into the best cakes and pies you ever tasted!

I always knew both of my grandmothers' and my great-aunt's food was special because everywhere there was a gathering—at a funeral, homecoming at the church, or a baby shower—folks wanted to know what Miss Nellie, Miss Daisy, and Miss Nervielee brought. No matter what else was on the table, it was their food that was the first to go. These Southern ladies took so much pride in this and really taught me well.

Miss Nellie—Mama Bishop to me—lived to be ninety-four years old. She made biscuits, corn bread, and pies, to name a few of her specialties. She taught me to roll dough when I was so young that I had to use my little yellow step stool to reach the counter. It never seemed to bother her if I made a mess with the flour. She knew it was all part of learning, making memories, and teaching me a skill I would be able to use forever and share with my own children.

Miss Daisy Bishop, my great-aunt, lived to be ninety-three years old. She was the cake baker.

The first stove she baked cakes in was a wood-burning one. Can you imagine? Even though she upgraded to a gas stove somewhere along the way, I can still see her sitting on a stool by the "new modern" stove, just to be sure that her cake stayed at the right temperature and didn't fall. On the rare occasion when one of her pound cakes would fall, Aunt Daisy would have a fit! But to me, the ones with the "sad" middle were especially yummy.

Miss Nervielee—Mama Adams to me—also lived to be ninety-four years old. She was an all-around exceptional cook and quite the gardener, too. Some of the produce that came out of her garden reminded me of the kind grown from radioactive seeds on the old television show *Gilligan's Island* (yes, I'm dating myself). Mama Adams stressed two things: one, the importance of eating fresh, healthy food, and two, cleanliness. I can still smell the bleach in her dishwater.

On Sundays after church, you could count on their kitchen tables being full of delicious food and a few desserts because they never knew who might stop by while out for a Sunday drive. The ladies wanted to show genuine hospitality to their visitors and tell them to come on in, pull up a chair, help themselves, and make themselves at home. There was always a "gracious plenty" of leftovers for supper, too. My grandmothers and great-aunt had an attitude of abundance. Though they were not wealthy, they were rich in the things that matter most: sharing love, showing kindness, and being grateful for a roof over their heads and good food on the table. It's no wonder they all lived into their nineties.

I feel so fortunate and truly blessed to have grown up in a family where having supper on the table was a priority, and being together to talk about the day was something everyone looked forward to. And I developed a deep love of baking from these talented women. The confidence they instilled in me is just what I needed—as well as tons of help from my mother—to get Daisy Cakes off the ground.

In June 2009, my mother and I started Daisy Cakes. Deciding which cakes to offer was the easy part. We had our family favorites of carrot, chocolate, coconut, and red velvet cakes down to a science. However, we quickly found out that trying to quadruple a cake recipe and make it in a 20-quart mixer is a far cry from making a single cake recipe in the 5-quart bowl of an electric stand mixer. It only took us three months to get it right! To say we went through a lot of butter, sugar, eggs, and milk before we figured it all out would be quite the understatement. Thank goodness for all of our friends and family, our guinea pigs who never seemed

to get tired of all the sampling we asked them to do.

During the three months of perfecting the recipes, there were several other details that had to be worked out: the name of the company, the size of the cakes, the source for the tins and labels, the shipping container design, and where to sell the cakes. I knew at least one of these decisions would be easy.

Fortunately, as a former member of the Junior League of Spartanburg, South Carolina, I was very familiar with the holiday shows that Junior League chapters put on as annual fund-raisers. Unfortunately, the registration deadline is in February or March, seven or eight months before the holiday shows begin. Here it was, almost the end of the summer, and I was just perfecting my recipes. Never one to shy away from a challenge or let a long-passed deadline stand in my way, I contacted the Junior Leagues of Lafayette and Baton Rouge, Louisiana, both of which have big holiday markets. I also reached out to the nation's biggest holiday fund-raiser, the Houston Ballet's Nutcracker Market. Being the extremely lucky person that I am, my mother and I and our new company, Daisy Cakes, got into all three events. Never underestimate the power of cake.

Our cake sales were $27,000 from September to December 2009. My mother and I couldn't have been happier with our new venture. While visiting these Southern cities, we made new friends and started building a customer base that would allow our business to grow. We were sharing family recipes with people who had the same appreciation for delicious, homemade desserts, along with similar childhood memories of learning to bake at the apron strings of their grandmothers and great-aunts. It was very rewarding.

Then came the summer of 2010. What a doozy it would turn out to be! It all started in June. I was sitting in my tiny office at my crowded little corner desk when the phone rang. The call was from an area code I didn't recognize, but the voice on the other end came through loud and clear. A good friend from high school (and college) was calling to tell me about this new television show I needed to be on called *Shark Tank*. Since I had not heard of the show, he explained it and encouraged me to apply. As soon as I hung up the phone, I went to the *Shark Tank* website and uploaded my information. Just as my (good) luck would have it, the casting coordinator called me the very next day! It was a long and productive summer that included lots of orders, baking, and many phone calls back and forth between Pauline, South Carolina, and Los Angeles. After a couple of very anxious months, I was finally deemed worthy to pitch in the "tank." The date was set for Halloween. The rest, as they say, is history.

Not enough can be said for the national recognition that comes from being on an Emmy Award–winning television show. Our sales went from two thousand cakes in 2010 to over twenty thousand cakes in 2016! But that's only part of the story. With the recognition came invitations to be on television shows and in magazines, and to have opportunities to meet and hang out with famous chefs. But I have to say that, for me, it's the letters and e-mails I've received from fans that make all the hard work worthwhile. So many people have shared stories about cooking with their grandmothers and said that my growing-up stories are so familiar to them. At food shows, I love talking to people about desserts, family recipes, and even their

ideas and inventions that one day may put them on *Shark Tank*. It's very humbling when someone asks to have a picture taken with me. It's a great feeling that warms my heart and makes me blush a little and smile really big!

This cookbook is for anyone with a sweet tooth who enjoys the creativity and personal satisfaction that goes along with baking something delicious and serving it to the "oohs" and "aahs" of family and friends. It's full of my family's favorite desserts, both old and new, as well as stories that set in motion my love for the organized chaos of a working kitchen. There are also baking hints, reminders, and words of wisdom mixed in that you'll find helpful, too.

A GRACIOUS PLENTY, DEFINED

If there's one phrase that describes not only my cooking style, but my family's entire cooking philosophy, it's "gracious plenty." It means to provide not only for everyone at the table, but really for anyone who might drop in or just show up—literally everyone and their brother! So when you see that a recipe makes "a gracious plenty" or that you have a "gracious plenty" left over, you can rest assured you'll have more than enough to go around.

I'm a big fan of mixing and matching cakes with frostings, fillings, and sauces, mostly because I can't help but think of all sorts of ways you can combine them. And so I've set up the recipes and chapters in a way that I hope helps you feel free enough to explore on your own. In the Cakes and Cupcakes chapter (page 19), whenever possible I've provided variations for the shape of cake you can make. For example, for the Chocolate Cake with White Frosting (page 25), the main recipe creates a 9-inch round layer cake. But you can also bake it as a sheet cake or cupcakes, so I've provided instructions on how to make those, too. And while the White Frosting is my personal favorite match for this cake, you can certainly give anything a whirl— like, for instance, Vanilla Buttercream Frosting (page 126), Whipped Cream (page 134), or Cream Cheese Frosting (page 123).

My pie recipes are similar, in that most of them have two or three ideas listed for a piecrust you can start with. But so many of the fillings are versatile, too. I give some options for how to tweak the fillings, but you should let your creativity run wild! Even the recipes in the Ice Creams and Puddings chapter (page 199) can be fillings for pies and cakes! Be sure to look out for my tips on using them in the most delicious ways.

The inspiration for this cookbook has come from all over the place—from making folks happy in my catering business and restaurants, to my cooking school and travels abroad. Whether your inspiration to bake comes from gathering eggs from pet hens, walking into a small family bakery in Europe, or watching your favorite chef on television, I hope this book will continue to excite your creativity in the kitchen. If you're new to baking, I hope my cookbook will ignite your passion to be fearless, to get into the kitchen, and to whip up your very first cake or batch of cookies. Inspiration comes from all walks of life, and being able to share that creativity in a yummy dessert—one you can really sink your teeth into (pun intended)—is what I find makes baking so much fun. This cookbook showcases how simple baking can be. Yes, it is first an exact science that requires precise mea-

suring (you can't just eyeball the ingredients), but once you can make a few simple recipes, you'll have the skills you need to venture on to new sauces, fillings, and frostings to make your desserts a little fancier or more decadent.

I hope you, along with your family and friends, will bake, share, and enjoy these recipes. Maybe you'll get a taste of what it was like going out on the front porch with a slice of cake or pie, sitting on the glider, catching a breeze, and waiting for the lightning bugs to come out.

some fun and interesting statistics

ON AVERAGE, EACH PERSON IN AMERICA ANNUALLY CONSUMES:

250 eggs

20.4 gallons of milk

5.6 pounds of butter

2.5 pounds of cream cheese

160 pounds of sugar

134 pounds of wheat flour

HERE'S WHAT WE USE AT DAISY CAKES ON AVERAGE EACH YEAR:

50,760 eggs

507 gallons of milk

9,720 pounds of butter

6,615 pounds of cream cheese

10,350 pounds of sugar

9,450 pounds of flour

We all need the proper tools to make any task at hand easier and more enjoyable. We need our tools of the trade, whatever our trade might be. A photographer needs a good camera and the necessary equipment that goes along with it to make beautiful photographs. An artist needs the proper brushes, paints, and pencils to create a masterpiece. The same holds true in the kitchen. If you are going to bake, there are a few necessary tools that will not only make the experience much more enjoyable, but also help the finished product turn out the way it is intended.

When I had my cooking school, Cooking Up a Storm, I couldn't emphasize enough to my students the importance of having quality ingredients and the appropriate things in which to prepare those ingredients. You can't expect a recipe to be completed properly without the right utensils, pots, and pans. Equipment doesn't have to be expensive either; there are plenty of good kitchen tools available at reasonable prices. Shop around and buy a few things along with way. Your baking experience will be a lot more satisfying, not to mention all the accolades you'll get from family and friends. And after all, isn't that what it's all about?

PEAR UPSIDE-DOWN CAKE, recipe on page 53

a few of my favorite baking things

MEASURING CUPS I prefer the heavy-duty ones with good, sturdy handles. I have not only the standard ¼-, ½-, ¾-, and 1-cup sizes, but also the ⅔-, 1½-, and 2-cup sizes as well.

MEASURING SPOONS Again, I prefer the heavy-duty ones. Of course, a standard set is a must for baking, but I also like having them for a pinch (typically ¹⁄₁₆ teaspoon), ⅛ teaspoon, ⅔ teaspoon, 1½ teaspoons, and 2 teaspoons.

BISCUIT CUTTERS I have a set of eleven cutters that nestle together, and I love them. The sizes range from 1 inch to 3½ inches. They come in a compact metal box that fits nicely in a drawer or cabinet.

ROLLING PIN I grew up using a rolling pin with ball bearings in the handle and I find this style easier to manipulate than other types. For rolling dough and biscuits, a good rolling pin is a must-have.

RUBBER SPATULAS I own several different kinds of spatulas. I prefer the flat rubber ones that are one piece of rubber from top to bottom. It's also good to have one or two heat-resistant ones that won't melt for making some sauces.

MICROPLANE ZESTER This is one of those utensils you don't want to be without. It's wonderful for cheeses, but when it comes to baking, it is a must for grating citrus, nutmeg, and chocolate.

PASTRY BRUSH Be sure to buy a good-quality pastry brush from a baking supply company. Otherwise, you risk the bristles coming out very easily in your food. If you are making your own pan grease (see Make Your Own Pan Grease, page 16), I recommend having a separate brush dedicated to it.

FLOUR-SACK TOWELS For making any of the log cakes (pages 55, 61–64), you'll need flour-sack towels for rolling the warm cake into a log shape.

CHEESECLOTH This is one of those things that takes up hardly any room in the drawer or cabinet and that you won't use very often. It is, however, one of those things that, when you need it, you don't want to be without. Cheesecloth is inexpensive, easy to find, and comes with a nice amount in the package, so it will last a long time.

CAKE PANS Both 8-inch and 9-inch cake pans are worth investing in. I recommend four of each, if you have the cabinet space. They stack!

SPRINGFORM CAKE PANS These cake pans have a clasp-release mechanism that unhinges so the sides of the pan fall away from the base without any trouble. Both 10-inch and 12-inch pans are what I use for cheesecakes since smaller pans can make for a mess in your oven if the filling overflows. A 9-inch pan is good to have for cheesecake recipes that call for less than three 8-ounce bricks of cream cheese and no-bake recipes that call for a springform pan.

JELLY ROLL AND HALF-SHEET PANS
Cakes, cookies, pies, and even ice cream turn out perfectly prepared in sheet pans. Since they fit nicely in the drawer under the stove, I recommend keeping three or four around. A half-sheet pan is 12 × 18 inches, while a true "jelly roll" is usually 11 × 15 inches.

TUBE PAN   You can't make a proper pound cake without one. Be sure you get the one *without* the removable bottom (used for angel food cake) or your batter will run out in your oven.

GLASS BAKING DISHES   These are great for cooking and baking, and they stack nicely in a cabinet, too. I like an 8 × 8 × 2-, 9 × 9 × 2-, 9 × 13 × 2-, and an 11 × 15 × 2-inch baking dish along with both 9- and 10-inch pie plates.

DOUBLE BOILER   This is the perfect pan for making custards. Cooking the eggs above the boiling water instead of directly on the burner will not only give you confidence making custards and curds but also ensure a perfectly smooth and delicious finished product. If you don't have a double boiler, a metal bowl set over a saucepan of simmering water works, too. Just be sure your bowl sits above—not in—the simmering water.

STAND MIXER   I can't imagine making a cake or other baked goods without one of these! Since a good mixer comes with three beater attachments, you can use the whisk for cake batter, the paddle for cookie dough and frostings, and the dough hook for bread doughs and biscuits. Even though it's expensive, a good-quality mixer is an investment that will last a lifetime.

MAKE YOUR OWN PAN GREASE

There's really no need to buy expensive nonstick spray when you can make your own "pan grease" for baking. This recipe is quick and easy to make, and it will keep in your fridge for up to three months. Since it's equal parts shortening, oil, and flour, you can make as little or as much as you need. I highly recommend preparing a big batch for your holiday baking!

∴ MAKES 2½ CUPS

1 cup vegetable shortening

1 cup canola oil

1 cup unbleached all-purpose flour

In the bowl of a stand mixer fitted with the whisk attachment, beat the shortening, oil, and flour on low speed until incorporated. Scrape down the sides and around the bottom of the bowl and continue beating on high speed until velvety smooth without any lumps, 3 minutes. The coating will keep in the fridge in an airtight container for up to 3 months. Whisk thoroughly before each use.

> It's very important to always read through the entire recipe before starting. That's the best way to avoid mistakes.

WHITE FROSTING, recipe on page 128

CAKES
and
cupcakes

I bake cakes nearly three hundred days a year. What I love about most cakes is how adaptable they are to almost every occasion. And that's exactly the way many of my cake recipes are written in this cookbook. If you need a layer cake, I've got you covered. If you need cupcakes, just make that same batter and put it into lined muffin tins. If it's a sheet cake you need to serve a crowd, that's in here, too, using the same reliable recipe.

When it comes to embracing your creative side, you can really mix it up by using your favorite batter in whatever pan or pans you need for the size of your party. I've included lots of delicious sauces, fillings, and frostings to choose from.

Cake is so versatile; it can be plain and simple or fancy and artistic. I hope you have fun making your own specialty desserts that will be enjoyed down to the last crumb.

This is the recipe that started it all! My mother and I first baked this all the way back in 1972, when we sold a four-layer yellow cake with chocolate frosting for a whopping seven dollars. Though it is a simple cake without all the bells and whistles of some of my other desserts, it is tried and true, and holds a very special place in my heart. However, if fancy is what you're looking for, you'll find lots of recipes throughout this book that you can use to really gussy these cakes layers right up—try the peach cake (the cover cake!) or caramel cake versions (see Variations), or Strawberry Sauce (page 137) as a filling between the layers with Vanilla Buttercream Frosting (page 126), Bacon Jam Filling with Bourbon (page 125) between the layers with Butterscotch Frosting (page 127), or, my personal favorite, Lemon Curd (page 145) between the layers with fresh lemon zest in Cream Cheese Frosting (page 123).

YELLOW CAKE
with chocolate frosting

∴ MAKES ONE 8-INCH 3-LAYER CAKE
    OR ONE 9-INCH 2-LAYER CAKE

Pan Grease (page 16) or extra vegetable shortening and flour for preparing the pans

1½ cups sugar

½ cup vegetable shortening

2 large eggs

1 tablespoon vegetable oil

2 cups sifted unbleached all-purpose flour

2¼ teaspoons baking powder

½ teaspoon salt

1 cup whole milk

1 teaspoon vanilla extract

Chocolate Frosting (page 118)

1   Preheat the oven to 350°F. Coat three 8-inch (or two 9-inch) round cake pans with Pan Grease (page 16) or a thin layer of shortening with a light dusting of flour.

2   In the bowl of a stand mixer fitted with the whisk attachment, beat together the sugar and shortening on high speed until fluffy, 3 minutes. Beat in the eggs and oil.

3   In a medium bowl, sift together the flour, baking powder, and salt. Add the flour mixture to the shortening mixture, along with the milk and vanilla. Beat on low speed until just combined, about 1 minute. Scrape down the sides and around the bottom of the bowl. Increase the speed to high and beat again for 1 more minute. Divide the batter evenly among the prepared pans.

4   Bake until the cake is golden and pulling away from the sides of the pans, 18 to 20 minutes. Let cool for 10 minutes before turning the layers out onto wire racks to cool completely.

5   Once cool, put one cake layer on a serving plate. Frost with ½ to ¾ cup of chocolate frosting. Add a second cake layer and spread with an additional ½ to ¾ cup of frosting. Add the final cake layer and frost the top and sides with the remaining frosting.

HINT Freezing the cake layers makes them much easier to frost. I usually freeze them for 2 to 3 hours, uncovered and flat on a sheet pan. Spreading the frosting over the frozen layers keeps the crumbs out.

recipe continues

Variations

PEACH CAKE   Add 1 cup of Peach Filling (page 196) to each cake layer along with Vanilla Buttercream Frosting (page 126). Serve with fresh peaches on the side.

CARAMEL CAKE   Add a teaspoon of caramel extract to the cake batter. Cut the cake layers in half (so you have 6 layers). Increase the recipe for the Caramel Frosting (page 119) by half and spread it between the layers before frosting the outside.

COCONUT, LEMON, OR ORANGE CAKE   Add 2 teaspoons of coconut, lemon, or orange extract to the batter. You can then frost it with Coconut Frosting (page 130), or lemon or orange frosting (see Variations, page 123).

YELLOW CUPCAKES   Line two cupcake pans with 18 liners. Divide the batter evenly among the liners, filling each two-thirds full. Bake in a 350°F oven until a toothpick inserted into the middle comes out with just a few crumbs on it, 18 to 20 minutes. Remove the cupcakes from the pan and let them cool completely on a wire rack. Frost and decorate as desired.

YELLOW SHEET CAKE   Grease and flour a 9 × 13 × 2-inch glass baking dish. Spread the batter evenly into the pan. Bake in a 350°F oven until golden brown and a toothpick inserted into the center of the cake comes out with just a few crumbs on it, 25 to 30 minutes. Cool completely and then cover with your favorite frosting.

For a thinner, larger cake, use a 12 × 18 × 1-inch half-sheet pan and bake for 20 to 22 minutes.

I grew up eating the leftover cherries that my mother didn't use in this beautiful cherry cake. Being an only child, I didn't have to worry about sharing them. The jars of cherries are a lot bigger these days, and the cherries are, too. I suggest buying the largest jar so there will be enough leftover cherries to go around; maybe even soak a few in a little moonshine (or bourbon; see page 172).

CHERRY CAKE

∴ MAKES ONE 8-INCH 3-LAYER CAKE OR
ONE 9-INCH 2-LAYER CAKE

1 Preheat the oven to 350°F. Coat three 8-inch (or two 9-inch) cake pans with Pan Grease (page 16) or shortening with a light dusting of flour.

2 In a small bowl, combine the milk, cherry juice, and vanilla. Set aside.

3 In the bowl of a stand mixer fitted with the whisk attachment, sift together the cake flour, sugar, baking powder, and salt. Drop in the shortening. Add half of the milk mixture. Beat on low speed for 2 minutes. Scrape down the sides and around the bottom of the bowl. Add the remaining milk mixture and the egg whites. Beat on low speed for 2 more minutes. Using a rubber spatula, fold in the cherries and pecans, if using. Divide the batter evenly among the prepared pans.

4 Bake until a toothpick inserted into the center of the cake comes out with just a few crumbs on it, 20 to 25 minutes. Let cool for 10 minutes before turning the layers out onto wire racks to cool completely.

5 Once cool, put one cake layer on a serving plate. Frost the top with the buttercream, add the second cake layer, and frost the top and sides.

Pan Grease (page 16) or extra vegetable shortening and flour for preparing the pans

¼ cup whole milk

½ cup maraschino cherry juice

1 teaspoon vanilla extract

2½ cups sifted cake flour

1½ cups sugar

3½ teaspoons baking powder

1 teaspoon salt

½ cup vegetable shortening

4 large egg whites

18 pitted maraschino cherries, well drained and finely chopped

½ cup chopped pecans (optional)

Vanilla Buttercream Frosting (page 126)

I absolutely adore anything chocolate! It is the ultimate comfort food and feel-good cake flavor. This recipe is as light and fluffy as they come. My favorite way to enjoy this cake is exactly the way I did when I was growing up and eating it at my neighbor's house: with lots of White Frosting (page 128) piled high on top. Thank you, Mary Alice, for letting me lick the beaters!

CHOCOLATE CAKE with white frosting

∴ MAKES ONE 9-INCH 3-LAYER CAKE

1 Preheat the oven to 350°F. Coat three 9-inch round cake pans with Pan Grease (page 16) or a thin layer of butter with a light dusting of cocoa powder.

2 In a medium bowl, sift together the flour, cocoa, baking powder, baking soda, and salt.

3 In the bowl of a stand mixer fitted with the whisk attachment, beat together the sugar and butter on high speed until fluffy, about 5 minutes. Scrape down the sides and around the bottom of the bowl. Beat in the eggs, egg yolk, oil, and vanilla. Add the flour mixture along with the warm water. Beat on low speed until blended. Scrape down the sides and around the bottom of the bowl. Increase the speed to high and beat for 1 minute. Divide the batter evenly among the prepared pans.

4 Bake until a toothpick inserted into the middle comes out with just a few crumbs on it, 22 to 24 minutes. Let cool for 10 minutes before turning the layers out onto wire racks to cool completely.

5 Once cool, put one cake layer on a serving plate. Frost the top with the white frosting, then add a second cake layer and frost the top. Add the final cake layer and frost the top and sides.

Pan Grease (page 16) or extra butter and Dutch-processed cocoa powder for preparing the pans

2¾ cups all-purpose flour

1 scant cup Dutch-processed cocoa powder

1 tablespoon baking powder

1 teaspoon baking soda

1 teaspoon salt

2¼ cups sugar

1 cup (2 sticks) unsalted butter, at room temperature

3 large eggs

1 large egg yolk

1 tablespoon vegetable oil

1 teaspoon vanilla extract

2 cups warm water (105°F to 110°F)

White Frosting (page 128)

recipe continues

Variations

CHOCOLATE MOUSSE CAKE   If you want a lighter frosting or filling, make a mousse-like filling by mixing a cup of fresh whipped cream with Chocolate Pudding (page 214) and only spread it between the layers and on the top of the cake, leaving the sides "naked."

CHOCOLATE CUPCAKES   Line two cupcake pans with 24 liners. Divide the batter evenly among the liners, filling each two-thirds full. Bake in a 350°F oven until a toothpick inserted into the middle comes out with just a few crumbs on it, 18 to 20 minutes. Remove the cupcakes from the pan and let cool completely on a wire rack. Frost and decorate as desired.

CHOCOLATE SHEET CAKE   Grease a 9 × 13 × 2-inch glass baking dish and dust with cocoa powder. Spread the batter evenly into the pan. Bake in a 350°F oven until a toothpick inserted into the center of the cake comes out with just a few crumbs on it, 28 to 30 minutes. Let cool completely and then cover with your favorite frosting.

For a thinner, larger cake, use a 12 × 18 × 1-inch half-sheet pan and bake for 20 to 25 minutes.

BLACK FOREST SHEET CAKE   For a three-layer rectangular cake, bake the cake in a 12 × 18 × 1-inch half-sheet pan for 25 to 30 minutes. Cut the layer into thirds, lengthwise. Brush the layers with cherry liqueur, spread a good-quality dark-cherry pie filling between the layers, and cover with White Frosting (page 128).

As I said during my pitch on Shark Tank, red velvet is a Southern holiday tradition. There are quite a few theories about the origin of this cake. Throughout my travels to food shows, where I often serve this cake to folks, I'm surprised by the number of people who say it's just a chocolate cake with red food coloring in it. I always feel the need to let them know "not where I come from!" One tablespoon of cocoa does not a chocolate cake make. When that bit of cocoa combines with a touch of vinegar, a lovely reddish hue results. Adding food coloring amps up the "wow" factor!

RED VELVET CAKE

⋮ MAKES ONE 9-INCH 3-LAYER CAKE

1 Preheat the oven to 350°F. Coat three 9-inch round cake pans with Pan Grease (page 16) or a thin layer of shortening with a light dusting of flour.

2 In a medium bowl, sift together the flour, cocoa, baking soda, salt, and baking powder.

3 In a small bowl, stir together the buttermilk, food coloring, vinegar, and vanilla.

4 In the bowl of a stand mixer fitted with the whisk attachment, beat together the sugar and butter on high speed until fluffy, 3 minutes. Reduce the speed to low and beat in the eggs. Scrape down the sides and around the bottom of the bowl. Beat thoroughly on high speed until smooth, 2 minutes. Add the flour mixture and the buttermilk mixture. Beat on low speed just until combined. Scrape the bowl again. Beat on high speed for 1 minute. Divide the batter evenly among the prepared pans.

5 Bake until a toothpick inserted into the center of each cake layer comes out clean, 18 minutes. The cakes will have pulled away from the edges of the pan, but the cakes' edges shouldn't be browned. Let cool for 10 minutes before turning the layers out onto wire racks to cool completely.

6 Once cool, put one cake layer on a serving plate. Frost the top with the cream cheese frosting, then add a second cake layer and frost the top. Add the final cake layer and frost the top and sides.

Pan Grease (page 16) or extra vegetable shortening and flour for preparing the pans

2½ cups unbleached all-purpose flour

1 tablespoon Dutch-processed cocoa powder

1½ teaspoons baking soda

½ teaspoon salt

¼ teaspoon baking powder

1 cup buttermilk (see Hint)

2 tablespoons red food coloring

1 tablespoon vinegar (white or balsamic)

1 teaspoon vanilla extract

2 cups sugar

½ cup (1 stick) unsalted butter, at room temperature

3 large eggs

Cream Cheese Frosting (page 123)

recipe continues

Variations

RED VELVET CUPCAKES   Line two cupcake pans with 24 liners. Divide the batter evenly among the liners, filling two-thirds full. Bake in a 350°F oven until a toothpick inserted into the middle comes out with just a few crumbs on it, 18 to 22 minutes. Remove the cupcakes from the pan and let cool completely on a wire rack. Frost and decorate as desired.

RED VELVET SHEET CAKE   Grease and flour a 9 × 13 × 2-inch glass baking dish. Spread the batter evenly in the pan. Bake in a 350°F oven until a toothpick inserted into the center of the cake comes out with just a few crumbs on it, 28 to 32 minutes. Let cool completely and then cover with your favorite frosting.

For a thinner, larger cake, use a 12 × 18 × 1-inch half-sheet pan and bake for 20 to 22 minutes. Cutting this cake in half and stacking the two layers makes a very pretty cake. It's lovely garnished with green and red cherries for the holidays.

> **HINT** If you don't have buttermilk, you can make your own. Just add 1 tablespoon white vinegar to 1 cup whole milk.

This is my go-to cake for all occasions. It's beautiful, delicious, and a crowd-pleaser. One year, at the South Beach Wine and Food Festival, I served 1,200 slices—from 100 pound cakes! My friends helped me dip the slices in melted butter before grilling them. After plating, we put a nice dollop of Lemon Curd (page 145) on each slice and topped it off with a Moonshine-Soaked Cherry (page 172). But I also love a slice all on its own with a cup of coffee.

miss daisy's
PLAIN POUND CAKE

·**:**· **MAKES ONE 10-INCH CAKE**

Pan Grease (page 16) or extra vegetable shortening and flour for preparing the pans

3 cups cake flour

½ teaspoon salt

1 cup vegetable shortening

¾ cup (1½ sticks) unsalted butter, at room temperature

3 cups sugar

6 large eggs

¾ cup whole milk

2 tablespoons vanilla extract

1　Preheat the oven to 350°F. Coat a 10-inch tube pan with Pan Grease (page 16) or a thin layer of shortening with a light dusting of flour.

2　In a medium bowl, sift together the cake flour and salt.

3　In the bowl of a stand mixer fitted with the whisk attachment, beat together the shortening, butter, and sugar on high speed until light and fluffy, 5 minutes. Beat in the eggs. Scrape down the sides and around the bottom of the bowl. Beat on high speed for 1 minute. Add the flour mixture along with the milk and vanilla, and beat well. Scrape down the sides and around the bottom of the bowl. Beat on high speed for 2 minutes. Pour the batter into the prepared tube pan and smooth out the top.

4　Bake until a toothpick inserted into the center comes out with just a few crumbs on it, 65 to 70 minutes. Let the cake cool for 20 minutes before removing it from the pan.

Hands down, without a doubt, this is my absolute favorite cake in the world! It is so moist and delicious, with an incredibly crunchy top. I swear, the longer you keep it, the better it gets! No mixer is required, so cleanup's a breeze.

APPLE-WALNUT POUND CAKE

∴ MAKES ONE 10-INCH CAKE

1 Preheat the oven to 350°F. Coat a 10-inch tube pan with Pan Grease (page 16) or a thin layer of shortening with a light dusting of flour.

2 In medium bowl, sift together the flour, baking soda, and salt.

3 In a large bowl, whisk together the sugar, oil, eggs, and vanilla until well blended and light yellow in color, 3 minutes. Whisk the flour mixture into the bowl; the batter will be very stiff. Using a spatula, fold in the apples, walnuts, and coconut. Spoon the batter into the prepared pan and spread evenly (it will be very thick).

4 Bake until a toothpick inserted into the center comes out clean, 1 hour and 20 minutes. Let the cake cool for 20 minutes before removing it from the pan.

Pan Grease (page 16) or extra vegetable shortening and flour for preparing the pans

3 cups unbleached all-purpose flour

1 teaspoon baking soda

1 teaspoon salt

2 cups sugar

1½ cups canola oil

3 large eggs

1 tablespoon vanilla extract

3 cups ½-inch pieces of peeled and cored apples (preferably Winesap)

1 cup black walnuts, coarsely chopped

1 cup sweetened coconut flakes

This is my mother's favorite cake recipe. Her best friend, Mabel, always made it for special occasions. It's a great cake for your holiday baking because you can make it ahead of time and freeze it. I am a firm believer that freezing this cake makes it even better! It's pretty garnished with red and green cherries, too.

miss geraldine's
ITALIAN CREAM CAKE

∴ MAKES ONE 9-INCH 3-LAYER CAKE

1 Preheat the oven to 350°F. Coat three 9-inch round cake pans with Pan Grease (page 16) or a thin layer of shortening with a light dusting of flour.

2 In the bowl of a stand mixer fitted with the whisk attachment, beat the egg whites on high speed until stiff, 3 minutes. Carefully transfer the whites to a clean, dry bowl and set aside.

3 In the same bowl used for the egg whites, whisk together the butter and the shortening on high speed for 2 minutes. Add the sugar and beat until light and fluffy, 5 minutes. Scrape down the sides and around the bottom of the bowl. Beat in the egg yolks on low speed to combine. Scrape down the bowl. Increase the speed to high and beat for 1 more minute.

4 Combine the baking soda and the buttermilk, stirring until dissolved. Pour the buttermilk into the butter mixture and add the flour. Beat on low speed for 30 seconds. Scrape down the sides and bottom of the bowl. Beat on high speed for 1 minute. Add the coconut, pecans, and both extracts. Mix well. Use a rubber spatula to fold in the beaten egg whites. Divide the batter among the prepared pans.

5 Bake until a toothpick inserted into the center of the cakes comes out with just a few crumbs on it, 25 minutes. Let the layers cool for 15 minutes before turning them out onto wire racks to cool completely.

6 Place one cake layer on a serving plate. Frost with ½ to ¾ cup Cream Cheese Frosting, then add a second cake layer and spread with ½ to ¾ cup frosting. Add the final cake layer and frost the top and sides.

Pan Grease (page 16) or extra vegetable shortening and flour for preparing the pans

5 large eggs, separated (see Hint)

½ cup (1 stick) unsalted butter, at room temperature

½ cup vegetable shortening

2 cups sugar

1 cup buttermilk

1 teaspoon baking soda

2 cups unbleached all-purpose flour, sifted twice

1 cup sweetened coconut flakes

1 cup chopped pecans

1 teaspoon vanilla extract

1 teaspoon coconut extract

Cream Cheese Frosting (page 123)

HINT Room-temperature egg whites whip up fluffier than cold ones straight from the fridge. That said, the colder the egg, the easier it is to separate the whites from the yolks. I like to separate cold eggs, put the whites into a small bowl, and then set that small bowl into a larger bowl of warm water for 10 minutes before beating.

Sometimes a big chunk of pound cake is just what the doctor ordered—especially if it's doused with a healthy pour of Buttered Rum Sauce! Be sure to start this recipe a day or two ahead of time to soak your raisins and to let the cake sit a while before serving. For an extra-special touch, try serving slices with some Roasted Pineapple (page 206).

RUM RAISIN POUND CAKE

∴ **MAKES ONE 10-INCH CAKE**

1   Combine the raisins and spiced rum and soak overnight, covered and at room temperature.

2   Preheat the oven to 250°F. Coat a 10-inch tube pan with Pan Grease (page 16) or a thin layer of butter with a light dusting of flour.

3   Drain the raisins. (Save the rum for the buttered rum sauce.) Pat the raisins dry and toss them with ¼ cup of the all-purpose flour in a colander.

4   In a medium bowl, sift together the remaining 3 cups flour, the baking powder, and salt.

5   In the bowl of a stand mixer fitted with the whisk attachment, beat together the butter, shortening, and sugar on high speed until fluffy, 3 minutes. Reduce the speed to low and beat in the eggs. Scrape down the sides and around the bottom of the bowl. Beat on high speed for 2 minutes. Add the flour mixture along with the milk and vanilla. Beat on low speed to combine. Scrape down the sides and around the bottom of the bowl. Beat on high speed for 1 minute. Using a rubber spatula, carefully fold in the raisins. Pour the batter into the prepared pan and smooth the top.

6   Bake the cake until it is golden brown and begins to pull away from the sides of the pan, about 2½ hours. During baking, *do not open the door or the cake will fall.* Remove the cake from the oven and cool in the pan for 20 minutes before turning it out onto a wire rack to cool completely.

7   After placing the cake on a serving plate, poke holes in the cake with a skewer and pour the warm rum sauce over the top. You can also serve the cake by the slice and drizzle the warm rum sauce over a piece at a time.

Pan Grease (page 16) or extra butter and flour for preparing the pan

2 cups raisins

1 cup spiced rum

3¼ cups unbleached all-purpose flour

1 teaspoon baking powder

½ teaspoon salt

1½ cups (3 sticks) unsalted butter, at room temperature

½ cup vegetable shortening

1½ cups sugar

4 large eggs

½ cup whole milk

1 teaspoon vanilla extract

Buttered Rum Sauce (page 135), warmed

HINT Soak the raisins in rum at least one day ahead of making the cake for the most flavorful, rum-infused taste. You can serve the cake right away, but I recommend covering the cake and letting it sit at room temperature for a day or two.

From the very beginning of Daisy Cakes, carrot cake has always been the number one seller. I like to think that this is because it's a super-moist cake and I use only one spice—cinnamon—and not too much of it. After all, it's not a spice cake. The carrots should be the star of the show, and using a pound of the sweet, orange beauties guarantees it! Feel free to use a little less or a tad more cinnamon, depending on how you like it.

CARROT CAKE

∴ MAKES ONE 8-INCH 3-LAYER CAKE
OR ONE 9-INCH 2-LAYER CAKE

Pan Grease (page 16) or extra vegetable shortening and flour for preparing the pan

2 cups unbleached all-purpose flour

1½ teaspoons baking soda

1 teaspoon baking powder

½ to 1 teaspoon ground cinnamon

¼ teaspoon salt

4 large eggs

1½ cups canola oil

2 cups sugar

1 pound carrots, shredded (2 cups)

1 8-ounce can crushed pineapple, drained

1 cup sweetened coconut flakes

½ cup chopped pecans

Cream Cheese Frosting (page 123)

1 Preheat the oven to 375°F. Coat three 8-inch (or two 9-inch) round cake pans with Pan Grease (page 16) or a thin layer of shortening with a light dusting of flour.

2 In a medium bowl, sift together the flour, baking soda, baking powder, cinnamon, and salt.

3 In a large bowl, whisk together the eggs, oil, and sugar until light yellow in color, 3 minutes. Stir in the carrots, pineapple, coconut, and pecans. Add the flour mixture and stir just until combined. Divide the batter evenly between the prepared pans.

4 Bake until the cake layers are pulling away from the sides of the pans and the middle springs back when touched, 45 to 50 minutes. Let cool for 15 minutes before turning the layers out onto wire racks to cool completely.

5 Once cool, put one cake layer on a serving plate. Frost the top with the cream cheese frosting, add the second cake layer, and frost the top and sides.

HINT Additional toasted, chopped pecans (see Hint, page 42) are quite pretty pressed onto the sides of the frosted cake.

Variation

CARROT CAKE CUPCAKES Line two cupcake pans with 24 liners. Divide the batter evenly among the liners, filling them two-thirds full. Bake in a 375°F oven until the cupcake centers spring back when gently touched, 25 to 28 minutes. Remove the cupcakes from the pan and let cool completely. Frost as desired.

*One of my fondest memories from growing up is the yearly trip
we'd take to the mountains to have a picnic and buy apples up near
Hendersonville, North Carolina. Mama Bishop, Mama Adams, Aunt
Daisy, my mother, and I would spend the entire day going from one
apple orchard to the other, looking for the perfect apples, tasting the
different varieties, and sipping lots of cool apple cider. During all of
those childhood mountain trips and even now, a Winesap apple has
been my favorite for eating and for baking.*

APPLE CAKE

·⁚· MAKES ONE 8-INCH 3-LAYER CAKE
OR ONE 9-INCH 2-LAYER CAKE

Pan Grease (page 16) or
extra vegetable shortening
and flour for preparing
the pan

2 cups unbleached
all-purpose flour

1 teaspoon baking powder

1 teaspoon baking soda

¼ teaspoon salt

4 large eggs

1½ cups canola oil

2 cups sugar

1 teaspoon vanilla extract

1 teaspoon caramel extract

3 to 4 medium sweet and
firm red apples, peeled,
halved, cored, and finely
chopped (about 2½ cups)

Cream Cheese Frosting
(page 123) or Caramel
Frosting (page 119)

1   Preheat the oven to 375°F. Coat three 8-inch (or two 9-inch) round
cake pans with Pan Grease (page 16) or a thin layer of shortening with
a light dusting of flour.

2   In a medium bowl, sift together the flour, baking powder, baking
soda, and salt.

3   In a large bowl, whisk together the eggs, oil, sugar, and both
extracts until light in color, 3 minutes. Stir in the apples. Add the
flour mixture and stir just until combined. Divide the batter evenly
between the prepared pans.

4   Bake until the cake layers are pulling away from the sides of the
pans and the middle springs back when touched, 35 to 40 minutes.
Let cool for 15 minutes before turning the layers out onto wire racks
to cool completely.

5   Once cool, put one cake layer on a serving plate. Spread with one
cup of the cream cheese frosting. Add the second cake layer, and
frost the top and sides with the remaining frosting.

Variations

APPLE MOONSHINE CAKE   For an adult version of this cake, brush each cake layer with 2 tablespoons of apple-pie-flavored moonshine (or any apple-flavored liqueur) before frosting.

CINNAMON APPLE CAKE   For cinnamon lovers, fold ¾ to 1 cup cinnamon chips into the batter before pouring it into the pans.

APPLE SHEET CAKE   Grease and flour a 9 × 13 × 2-inch glass baking dish. Pour the batter into the prepared pan. Bake in a 350°F oven until the middle of the cake springs back when touched, 38 to 40 minutes. Let cool completely and then frost. This cake is pretty cut in half lengthwise, stacked and frosted as a rectangular layer cake, and covered in chopped, toasted pecans.

For a thinner, larger cake, use a 12 × 18 × 1-inch half-sheet pan and bake for 30 to 35 minutes.

I remember the first time I had this cake at a friend's birthday party during junior high school. The cake reminded me of my favorite ice cream, rocky road. I could have eaten the entire mud cake by myself— at thirteen years old, I remember thinking it was the best combination of ingredients I had ever tasted! Thank you, Mrs. Foster, for introducing me to one of my very favorite desserts.

MISSISSIPPI MUD CAKE

∴ **MAKES ONE 11 × 15-INCH SHEET CAKE**

1 Preheat the oven to 350°F. Butter an 11 × 12 -inch glass baking dish, and dust with 2 tablespoons cocoa powder.

2 In a large bowl, whisk together the sugar, flour, baking soda, and salt.

3 In a medium saucepan set over medium heat, whisk together the milk, butter, and the remaining ¾ cup cocoa until the butter is melted and the mixture is smooth, 7 to 8 minutes. Remove the saucepan from the heat. Add the vanilla and whisk the mixture into the flour mixture.

4 In a small bowl, whisk the eggs well. Stir them into the flour and milk mixture. Spread the batter into the prepared pan. Sprinkle with the chocolate chips.

5 Bake until a toothpick inserted into the center comes out clean, 30 to 34 minutes. Remove the pan from the oven and sprinkle the marshmallows and toasted pecans evenly over the top of the cake. Pour the ganache over the marshmallows and pecans, being careful to keep them evenly spread across the top of the cake. Cover and refrigerate overnight before serving.

> **HINT** To toast nuts: Spread the nuts out evenly on a rimmed baking sheet. Bake at 350°F for 7 minutes for lightly toasted pecans, or 9 to 10 minutes for a deeper roast. If using sliced and slivered almonds, they should be checked after 5 minutes, as they toast faster.

1 cup (2 sticks) unsalted butter, plus more for greasing the pan

¾ cup plus 2 tablespoons Dutch-processed cocoa powder

2¼ cups sugar

2 cups unbleached all-purpose flour

1 teaspoon baking soda

½ teaspoon salt

1½ cups whole milk

1 teaspoon vanilla extract

2 large eggs

1 cup semisweet chocolate chips

2 cups miniature marshmallows

1 cup chopped pecans, toasted (see Hint)

¼ recipe Chocolate Ganache (page 132), made with semisweet chocolate

One summer, my family and I went on vacation to Scotland, where I ate haggis every day and enjoyed truly the best fish-and-chips in the world in the lovely little seaside town of Anstruther. On the short drive from Anstruther back to St. Andrews, a pasture full of Holstein-Friesian cows caught our eye. We just had to stop. Turns out, they were grazing in the pasture of a dairy that had a restaurant. Stuffed though we may have been, we just couldn't keep ourselves from buying some fresh cheeses and several desserts. This one was our favorite. Thank you for the recipe, St. Andrews Farmhouse Cheese Company!

Butter, for greasing the pan

1¼ cups sugar, plus 1 tablespoon for dusting the pan

¾ cup ground almonds or almond meal, plus 1 tablespoon for dusting

3 medium unpeeled navel oranges

½ teaspoon baking powder

9 large eggs

SCOTLAND ORANGE CAKE

∴ **MAKES ONE 12-INCH CAKE**

1   Preheat the oven to 350°F. Generously butter a 12-inch springform pan and dust with 1 tablespoon sugar and 1 tablespoon ground almonds.

2   Put the whole oranges in a medium saucepan, add ½ cup of the sugar, and cover with cold water. Bring to a boil over medium-high heat. Cover and simmer until tender, about 1 hour. Drain the oranges (discard the liquid). When cool, quarter the oranges and remove and any seeds. Put the oranges in a food processor fitted with the blade attachment and puree until smooth.

3   In a medium bowl, combine the remaining ¾ cup ground almonds, the remaining ¾ cup sugar, and the baking powder.

4   In the bowl of a stand mixer fitted with the whisk attachment, beat the eggs on high speed until thick and creamy, 5 to 6 minutes. Using a rubber spatula, fold in the orange puree just until combined. Carefully fold in the almond mixture until smooth. Pour the batter into the prepared pan.

5   Bake until the cake is firm and a knife inserted into the center comes out clean, 45 minutes. Let cool and then cover and refrigerate for 4 hours or overnight before removing from the pan and serving.

This is about as easy and simple a coffee cake as you can find. It's incredibly versatile, and I've included some of my favorite filling and glaze combinations for you to try out. But don't be afraid to experiment with other ideas to make it your very own.

YOUR SIGNATURE COFFEE CAKE

∴ MAKES ONE 8 × 8-INCH CAKE

1   Preheat the oven to 350°F. Grease and lightly flour an 8 × 8 × 2-inch glass baking dish.

2   In a medium bowl, sift together the flour, baking powder, and salt.

3   In the bowl of a stand mixer fitted with the whisk attachment, beat the butter and sugar on high speed until light and fluffy, 3 minutes. Beat in the eggs. Scrape down the sides and around the bottom of the bowl. Beat on high for 1 minute. Add the flour mixture, milk, and vanilla. Beat on low speed just until moistened. Spread a third of the batter over the bottom of the pan. Spoon half of your filling choice evenly over the batter, leaving about an inch or so of the border empty. Carefully spread another third of the batter over the filling, and then top with the remaining filling. Cover with the remaining batter, and sprinkle with the topping or drizzle with the glaze of your choice.

4   Bake until golden brown and a toothpick inserted into the center comes out with just a few crumbs on it, 40 to 45 minutes. Serve warm.

½ cup (1 stick) unsalted butter, at room temperature, plus more for greasing the pan

2 cups unbleached all-purpose flour

2 teaspoons baking powder

¾ teaspoon salt

1½ cups sugar

2 large eggs

1 cup whole milk

1 teaspoon vanilla extract

Filling and glaze combination of your choice (recipes follow)

BLUEBERRY FILLING
with lemon glaze

For the filling, in a food processor fitted with the blade attachment, pulse 2 cups fresh blueberries with ¼ cup (packed) light brown sugar and the zest of 1 lemon until coarsely chopped.

For the glaze, in a small bowl, whisk together 1½ cups confectioners' sugar, 1 tablespoon whole milk, and 2 teaspoons fresh lemon juice from the zested lemon.

recipe continues

CRANBERRY FILLING
with orange glaze

For the filling, in a food processor fitted with the blade attachment, pulse 2 cups fresh cranberries with ½ cup (packed) light brown sugar and the zest of 1 orange until coarsely chopped.

For the glaze, in a small bowl, stir together ¾ cup confectioners' sugar, 1 tablespoon whole milk, and 2 teaspoons fresh orange juice.

> **HINT** If you're in a hurry and feel like you just can't do one more thing, melt half of a 12- or 13-ounce jar of orange marmalade in a small saucepan over medium heat. When your cranberry coffee cake comes out of the oven, brush the top with the orange marmalade glaze. Your secret is safe with me.

PEACH FILLING
with pecan topping

For the filling, chop enough thawed frozen peaches to yield 2 cups. In a medium bowl, toss the chopped peaches with ½ cup (packed) light brown sugar and ⅛ teaspoon ground cinnamon, if desired. Let sit for 30 minutes. Drain before using.

For the topping, in a small bowl, combine ½ cup chopped pecans, ¼ cup (packed) light brown sugar, 6 tablespoons (¾ stick) cubed unsalted butter, and a pinch of ground cinnamon, if desired. Using your fingertips, mix until coarse. Sprinkle evenly over the batter before baking.

STRAWBERRY FILLING
with almond topping

For the filling, in a small bowl, toss 2 cups sliced fresh strawberries with ¼ cup sugar and let stand for 30 minutes. Drain before using.

For the topping, in a small bowl, combine ½ cup slivered almonds, ¼ cup (packed) light brown sugar, ¼ cup all-purpose flour, and ¼ cup (½ stick) cubed unsalted butter. Using your fingertips, mix until coarse. Sprinkle evenly over the batter before baking.

Moist cake with a surprise filling and a drizzle of rich ganache makes these cupcakes truly out of this world! Don't enjoy them just for dessert. They are perfect with a cup of coffee in the morning or with a nice cup of hot tea in the afternoon. They also freeze beautifully, so you can make them ahead and put them on the table for guests over a holiday weekend. You'll need two cupcake pans if you want to bake the full recipe—if you have only one 12-cup pan, then the recipe can be reduced by half.

BANANA CUPCAKES

∴ **MAKES 24 CUPCAKES**

FILLING

1 8-ounce package cream cheese, at room temperature

¼ cup sugar

1 large egg

1 teaspoon vanilla extract

1 cup semisweet chocolate chips or finely chopped, toasted pecans

1 recipe Banana Cake batter (page 54)

¼ recipe Chocolate Ganache (page 132), made with semisweet chocolate

1   **Make the filling:** In the bowl of a stand mixer fitted with the paddle attachment, beat the cream cheese and sugar on medium speed until well blended, 2 minutes. Add the egg and vanilla, and beat on high speed for 1 minute. Scrape down the sides and around the bottom of the bowl. With the mixer on the lowest speed, pour in the chocolate chips and beat until incorporated, 30 seconds.

2   Preheat the oven to 375°F. Line two cupcake pans with 24 liners.

3   Divide half the Banana Cake batter evenly among the liners (I like to scrape the batter into a large liquid measuring cup and then scoop out half of the batter, adding it to a medium bowl—I'll use this batter in the bowl to divide among the liners). Drop 1 heaping teaspoon of the cream cheese filling into each of the cupcakes. Cover the filling with the remaining batter.

4   Bake until a toothpick inserted into the middle comes out with a few crumbs on it, 22 to 24 minutes. Remove the cupcakes from the pan and let cool completely before drizzling with the ganache.

Variation

SPIKED BANANA CUPCAKES   After cooling the cupcakes completely, try brushing them with a little banana liqueur before drizzling with ganache.

I love the way gingerbread—with its delicious combination of cinnamon, ginger, cloves, and molasses—makes the kitchen smell festive during the holidays, so I came up with another reason to bake it. Here, I added pears, which makes this cake super moist, while the cast-iron skillet gives it a chewy edge that's to die for.

PEAR UPSIDE-DOWN CAKE

∴ MAKES ONE 10-INCH CAKE

1 Prepare the pears: Melt the butter in a cast-iron skillet set over medium heat. Sprinkle the brown sugar over the melted butter. Without stirring, allow the sugar to partially melt, 3 minutes. Place the pears, cut-side down, in the skillet and let cook for 3 minutes. Carefully turn the pears over so the cut side is facing up and arrange them evenly in a spoke design with the thinner stem end toward the middle of the skillet and the fatter end facing the outside. Cook until the pears start to sizzle, 2 minutes. Remove the pan from the heat.

2 Preheat the oven to 350°F.

3 Make the cake: In a medium bowl, sift together the flour, baking soda, ginger, cinnamon, cloves, and salt.

4 In the bowl of a stand mixer fitted with the whisk attachment, beat together the butter, egg, and molasses on high speed for 1 minute. Scrape down the sides and around the bottom of the bowl. Beat on high speed for 1 more minute. Add the sifted flour mixture along with the boiling water. Beat on low speed just to combine. Scrape down the sides and around the bottom of the bowl. Beat on high speed for 30 seconds. Carefully pour the batter over the pears, keeping them in the spoke pattern.

5 Bake until a tester inserted into the middle comes out clean, 45 to 50 minutes. Let the cake cool on a rack for 15 minutes before loosening the edges and turning it out onto a rimmed cake plate. Serve warm or at room temperature.

PEARS

⅓ cup (6 tablespoons) unsalted butter

¾ cup (packed) light brown sugar

4 Anjou or Bartlett pears, peeled, halved, and cored (it's best if all of the pears are about the same size)

CAKE

2½ cups unbleached all-purpose flour

1½ teaspoons baking soda

1 teaspoon ground ginger

½ teaspoon ground cinnamon

¼ teaspoon ground cloves

¼ teaspoon salt

½ cup (1 stick) unsalted butter, at room temperature

1 large egg

1 cup unsulphured molasses

1 cup boiling water

My mother and I opened our first restaurant in July 1990. This banana cake was one of our most popular desserts. We had customers who came to lunch only on the days we had this banana cake. It is super moist and not too sweet—a perfect combo!

BANANA CAKE

∴ MAKES ONE 8-INCH 3-LAYER CAKE OR
ONE 9-INCH 2-LAYER CAKE

1   Preheat the oven to 375°F. Coat three 8-inch (or two 9-inch) round cake pans with Pan Grease (page 16) or a thin layer of shortening with a light dusting of flour.

2   In a medium bowl, sift together the flour, baking powder, baking soda, and salt.

3   In a large bowl, whisk together the eggs, oil, buttermilk, sugar, and vanilla until light in color, 3 minutes. Stir in the bananas. Add the flour mixture and stir just until combined. Divide the batter evenly between the prepared pans.

4   Bake until the cake layers are pulling away from the sides of the pans and the middle springs back when touched, 35 to 40 minutes. Let cool for 15 minutes before turning the layers out onto wire racks to cool completely.

5   Once cool, put one cake layer on a serving plate. Frost the top with the whipped cream, add a second cake layer, and frost the top and sides.

Variation

BANANA PUDDING CAKE   For banana pudding lovers, divide each cake layer in half for four layers and fill with 2 cups of Vanilla Pudding (page 209) combined with 1 cup of Whipped Cream (page 134). Frost the sides and top of the cake with more whipped cream.

Pan Grease (page 16) or extra vegetable shortening and flour for preparing the pan

2 cups unbleached all-purpose flour

1 teaspoon baking powder

1 teaspoon baking soda

¼ teaspoon salt

4 large eggs

¾ cup canola oil

¾ cup buttermilk

2 cups sugar

1 teaspoon vanilla extract

3 cups mashed ripe bananas (5 to 6 medium)

Whipped Cream (page 134)

Also known as a chocolate yule log, this is a classic French Christmas-time treat. The French teacher at my children's elementary school always asked me to bake this cake for her students to enjoy during the holiday season. It is not too difficult to make, if you have the proper equipment: a 12 × 18 × 1-inch half-sheet pan and a large flour-sack towel. Don't let rolling the cake scare you. It's really a fun cake to bake and decorate. For me, the smiles on the children's faces make it all worthwhile.

BÛCHE DE NOËL

⋰ **MAKES ONE 12-INCH LOG CAKE**

1   Preheat the oven to 325°F. Grease a 12 × 18 × 1-inch half-sheet pan with butter or shortening and line it with parchment paper. Grease the parchment paper with butter or shortening and dust lightly with Dutch-processed cocoa powder.

2   **Make the cake:** In a medium bowl, sift together the flour, the remaining ocoa, and salt.

3   In the bowl of a stand mixer fitted with the whisk attachment, beat the egg yolks until thick and lemon colored, 5 minutes. Add ½ cup of the sugar and the vanilla. Beat on high speed for an additional 2 minutes. Add the flour mixture and beat on low speed for 1 minute. Scrape down the sides and around the bottom of the bowl. Increase the speed to high and beat for 30 seconds. Transfer the batter to a separate bowl while beating the egg whites.

4   Wash and fully dry the mixer bowl and whisk, then, in the clean bowl, beat the egg whites on high speed until frothy, 1 minute. Add the cream of tartar and beat on high speed until stiff, 2 minutes. With the mixer still running, gradually add the remaining ½ cup sugar and continue beating the egg whites until the peaks are very stiff and glossy, 2 minutes.

5   Gently fold the egg white mixture into the flour mixture just until combined. Spread the batter evenly into the prepared pan.

6   Bake until the cake springs back when touched, 22 to 24 minutes. Let the cake cool in the pan for 10 minutes.

CAKE

Butter or shortening for the pan

¼ cup Dutch-processed cocoa powder, plus additional for the pan

6 tablespoons unbleached all-purpose flour

¼ teaspoon salt

6 large eggs, separated

1 cup granulated sugar

1 teaspoon vanilla extract

½ teaspoon cream of tartar

¼ cup confectioners' sugar, for rolling

CREAM FILLING

1 cup heavy whipping cream

¼ cup confectioners' sugar

½ teaspoon vanilla extract

Chocolate Frosting (page 118)

Chocolate Sauce (page 138)

recipe continues

7   Lay a flour-sack towel that is the same size or larger than the cake pan on your work surface (see the photo on page 62). Use a fine-mesh sieve to sprinkle 2 tablespoons of the confectioners' sugar over the towel. Be sure not to let the cake sit for longer than 10 minutes or it may break when you try to roll it. Turn the warm cake out of the pan onto the prepared flour-sack towel. Remove the parchment paper and sprinkle the cake with the remaining 2 tablespoons confectioners' sugar. From one short end to the other, roll up the cake, keeping the towel inside it as you roll to keep the cake from sticking together. Let cool completely in the towel before unrolling the cake to spread with cream filling.

8   **Prepare the filling:** Put the bowl of a stand mixer and the whisk attachment in the freezer for 5 minutes before starting.

9   In the cold bowl of the stand mixer, beat the cream, confectioners' sugar, and vanilla on high speed until stiff, 3 to 4 minutes.

10 Unroll the cooled cake onto wax paper and remove the towel. Spread the cream filling onto the cooled cake. Reroll the cake carefully, lay the towel over the cake, and refrigerate for at least 1 hour.

11 Spread the chilled cake with the chocolate frosting. Slice and serve with the chocolate sauce.

Variation

MINTY BÛCHE DE NOËL   You can substitute ½ teaspoon mint extract for the vanilla in the cream filling, and garnish the outside of the frosted yule log with small pieces of broken peppermints.

One summer, several friends and I went on a three-week trip to Italy. To say we ate and drank a lifetime of deliciousness in twenty-one days would be an understatement. One of our favorite towns was Luciano, where we took several authentic Italian cooking classes. This is one of the desserts Fabrizio, our instructor, taught us.

TUSCAN FLAT CAKE

∴ **MAKES ONE 11 × 15-INCH SHEET CAKE**

1 cup plus ½ teaspoon granulated sugar

1 cup warm water (110°F to 115°F)

1 tablespoon active dry yeast

Pan Grease (page 16) or extra vegetable shortening and flour for preparing the pans

3¼ cups unbleached all-purpose flour

⅔ cup vegetable shortening

4 large egg yolks

Grated zest of 1 medium orange

1 teaspoon vanilla extract

Pinch of salt

Confectioners' sugar, for dusting

1   In a small bowl, dissolve the ½ teaspoon granulated sugar in the warm water. Stir in the yeast until it is completely dissolved. Let sit until the mixture foams, 5 to 10 minutes.

2   Coat an 11 × 15 × 2-inch baking pan with Pan Grease (page 16) or a thin layer of shortening with a light dusting of flour.

3   Put the flour in the bowl of a stand mixer fitted with the paddle attachment and add the yeast mixture. Beat on low speed until the dough is firm and easily pulls away from the sides of the bowl, 3 minutes. Cover and let rise in a warm place until doubled in size, 1 hour.

4   In a medium bowl, combine the remaining 1 cup granulated sugar, shortening, egg yolks, orange zest, vanilla, and salt. Add this mixture to the dough and beat on low speed until thoroughly blended, 3 minutes.

5   Evenly press the dough into the baking pan to a 1-inch thickness. Cover the dough and let it rise again in a warm place until doubled in size, 2 hours.

6   Preheat the oven to 350°F. Uncover the dough and bake until golden brown, 25 to 30 minutes. Let the cake cool for 15 to 20 minutes before turning it out onto a rectangular cake platter and dusting with confectioners' sugar. The cake can be served whole or cut into individual pieces.

HINT   The cake needs time to rise. You can bake it a day ahead and store in an airtight container. Before serving, dust it with confectioners' sugar.

When late spring and early summer arrive and the strawberries and peaches start to come in, it's the perfect time of year for this cake. A little fruit filling rolled up inside this sweet crumb is a lovely way to welcome back the warm weather.

VANILLA CAKE ROLL

.⋮. **MAKES ONE 12-INCH LOG CAKE**

1 Preheat the oven to 325°F. Grease a 12 × 18 × 1-inch half-sheet pan with butter or shortening and line with parchment paper. Grease the parchment paper with butter or shortening and dust lightly with flour.

2 In the bowl of a stand mixer fitted with the whisk attachment, beat the cold water and egg yolks on high speed until pale yellow and stiff, 5 minutes. Add the vanilla and sugar. Beat on high for 1 minute.

3 Sift together the flour, baking powder, and salt. Fold into the egg mixture. Transfer to a separate bowl.

4 Wash and fully dry the mixer bowl and whisk, then beat the egg whites on high speed until stiff, 3 minutes. Gently fold the egg whites into the flour mixture until completely combined. Spread the batter evenly into the prepared pan.

5 Bake until the cake is golden brown and the top springs back when touched, 15 to 18 minutes and set aside to cool for no longer than 10 minutes. (If left for longer, the cake may break when you try to roll it.)

6 Lay a flour-sack towel that is the same size or larger than the cake pan on your work surface (see photo on page 62). Use a fine-mesh sieve to sprinkle 2 tablespoons of the confectioners' sugar over the towel. Turn the warm cake out of the pan onto the prepared flour-sack towel. Remove the parchment paper and sprinkle the cake with the remaining 2 tablespoons confectioners' sugar. From one short end to the other, roll up the cake, keeping the towel inside it as you roll to keep the cake from sticking together. Let cool completely in the towel before unrolling the cake to spread with filling.

Butter or vegetable shortening for greasing the pan

1½ cups unbleached all-purpose flour, plus more for the pan

¾ cup cold water

4 large eggs, separated

1 teaspoon vanilla extract

1¼ cups granulated sugar

1 teaspoon baking powder

¼ teaspoon salt

¼ cup confectioners' sugar, for dusting

Peaches Foster (page 142)

Whipped Cream (page 134)

recipe continues

7 Unroll the cooled cake onto waxed paper, remove the towel, and spread it with the peach filling. Roll the cake back up and frost it with the fresh whipped cream. Refrigerate for 3 hours or overnight.

Variation

LEMONY CAKE ROLL Substitute 1 teaspoon lemon extract for the vanilla in the batter. Fill the cake with Lemon Curd (page 145) before frosting it with Whipped Cream (page 134) or Cream Cheese Frosting (page 123).

Here in the South, we love our pecans. I particularly love them in this log cake, which is light, delicate, and perfect for a luncheon or shower. It really fits the bill and has been a favorite in my family for years. Rolled in and dusted with confectioners' sugar, it's a fun cake to make, too.

PECAN ROLL

·:· **MAKES ONE 12-INCH LOG CAKE**

Butter or vegetable shortening and flour for the pan

7 large eggs, separated

¾ cup granulated sugar

1½ cups ground pecans

1 teaspoon baking powder

¼ teaspoon salt

6 tablespoons confectioners' sugar

½ recipe Whipped Cream (page 134)

1 Preheat the oven to 350°F. Grease a 12 × 18 × 1-inch half-sheet pan with butter or shortening and line with parchment paper. Grease the parchment with butter or shortening and dust with flour.

2 In the bowl of a stand mixer fitted with the whisk attachment, beat the egg whites on high speed until stiff and glossy peaks form, 4 minutes. Transfer to a bowl.

3 Beat the egg yolks and granulated sugar on high speed in the bowl used to beat the whites until pale and falling in ribbons when the beater is lifted, 10 minutes.

4 Meanwhile, in a small bowl, stir together the ground pecans, baking powder, and salt. Stir the pecan mixture into the egg yolk mixture. Fold in the stiffly beaten egg whites. Spread the batter evenly into the prepared pan.

5 Bake until golden brown, 15 to 20 minutes and set aside to cool for no longer than 10 minutes. (If left for longer, the cake may break when you try to roll it.)

6 Lay a flour-sack towel that is the same size or larger than the cake pan on your work surface (see photo on page 62). Use a fine-mesh sieve to sprinkle 2 tablespoons of the confectioners' sugar over the towel. Turn the warm cake out of the pan onto the prepared flour-sack towel. Remove the parchment paper and sprinkle the cake with 2 tablespoons confectioners' sugar. From one short end to the other, roll up the cake, keeping the towel inside it as you roll to keep the cake from sticking together. Refrigerate for 2 to 3 hours.

7 Remove the cake from the refrigerator and let it cool completely in the towel. Once cool, carefully unroll it onto waxed paper and remove the towel. Spread the whipped cream over the cake. Reroll the cake and sprinkle it with the remaining 2 tablespoons confectioners' sugar. If you're not serving this cake right away, be sure to have some confectioners' sugar on hand for a last-minute sprinkle.

I can't think of anything better after Thanksgiving dinner than a light and refreshing dessert, and this pretty pumpkin roll is just right. Served cool from the fridge, it can be made a day or two ahead of time. It can stand alone the Whipped Pumpkin Filling, or spread the outside with Whipped Cream before serving. Either way, you simply can't keep your fork out of this retro dessert.

PUMPKIN ROLL

∴ **MAKES ONE 12-INCH LOG CAKE**

1   Preheat the oven to 375°F. Grease a 12 × 18 × 1-inch half-sheet pan with butter or shortening and line with parchment paper. Grease the parchment paper with butter or shortening and dust lightly with flour.

2   In a medium bowl, sift together the flour, pumpkin pie spice, baking powder, baking soda, and salt.

3   In the bowl of a stand mixer fitted with the whisk attachment, beat the eggs and sugar on high speed until pale yellow and thickened, 3 minutes. Add the pumpkin and vanilla. Beat on high speed for 1 minute. Using a rubber spatula, carefully fold in the flour mixture just until combined. Spread the batter evenly into the prepared pan.

4   Bake until the top of the cake springs back when touched, 10 to 12 minutes and set aside for no longer than 10 minutes. (If left for longer, the cake may break when you try to roll it.)

5   Lay a flour sack towel that is the same size or larger than the cake pan on your work surface (see the photo on page 62). Use a fine-mesh sieve to sprinkle 2 tablespoons of the confectioners' sugar over the towel. Turn the warm cake out of the pan onto the prepared flour-sack towel. Remove the parchment paper and sprinkle the cake with the remaining 2 tablespoons confectioners' sugar. From one short end to the other, roll up the cake, keeping the towel inside it as you roll to keep the cake from sticking together. Let cool completely in the towel before unrolling the cake to spread with cream filling.

6   Unroll the cooled cake, remove the towel, and spread it with the whipped pumpkin filling. Roll the cake back up and refrigerate, covered with plastic wrap. When ready to serve, spread with whipped cream, if desired.

Butter or vegetable shortening for greasing the pan

¾ cup unbleached all-purpose flour, plus more for the pan

½ to 1 teaspoon pumpkin pie spice

½ teaspoon baking powder

½ teaspoon baking soda

¼ teaspoon salt

3 large eggs

1 cup granulated sugar

¾ cup 100% pure pumpkin puree

2 teaspoons vanilla extract

¼ cup confectioners' sugar, for dusting

Whipped Pumpkin Filling (page 140)

Whipped Cream (page 134, optional)

If your Thanksgiving morning is all about enjoying the Macy's Thanksgiving Day Parade, then your Thanksgiving afternoon should be all about waking from your nap to a big slice of this cold and creamy cheesecake. The only thing you'll want to add is a little dollop of whipped cream or caramel sauce (page 121) with a swig of bourbon on the side.

PUMPKIN CHEESECAKE

·⋰· **MAKES ONE 12-INCH CHEESECAKE**

1 **Make the crust:** Grease a 12-inch springform pan with butter and set aside. In a food processor fitted with the blade attachment, pulse the cookies until the mixture is coarse like cornmeal. Add the brown sugar and pulse until blended. With the food processor running, slowly pour in the melted butter and process until combined, 30 seconds. Press the cookie mixture into the prepared pan. Wrap the outside of the pan in foil, covering the bottom and halfway up the sides to prevent any butter in the crust dripping into the oven.

2 Preheat the oven to 350°F.

3 **Prepare the filling:** In the bowl of a stand mixer fitted with the paddle attachment, beat the cream cheese on high speed until smooth, 3 minutes. Add the pumpkin and beat until combined. Beat in the sugars, flour, and salt. Add the eggs and beat until combined. Scrape down the sides and around the bottom of the bowl. Beat on high speed until smooth, 2 minutes. Add the cream and vanilla, and beat on low speed 1 minute. Scrape down the sides and around the bottom of the bowl. Beat until smooth, 1 more minute. Pour the filling over the crust. Gently shake the pan back and forth to evenly spread the filling.

4 Bake until the cheesecake is firm, the top is slightly cracked, and a knife inserted into the center comes out clean, 1½ hours. Let cool completely. Refrigerate overnight for best results before removing from the pan.

CRUST

½ cup (1 stick) unsalted butter, melted, plus more for the pan

1 11-ounce bag gingersnap cookies

¼ cup (packed) dark brown sugar

FILLING

3 8-ounce packages cream cheese, at room temperature

1 15-ounce can 100% pure pumpkin puree

1 cup granulated sugar

¼ cup (packed) dark brown sugar

¼ cup unbleached all-purpose flour

¼ teaspoon salt

4 large eggs

½ cup heavy whipping cream

1 tablespoon vanilla extract

For nearly two years, my mother and I baked cheesecakes for a local restaurant. We wanted to be sure they had a good variety, so we came up with a recipe that would bake nicely with different ingredients added to the base. We varied what coarsely chopped pieces of cookies or candy bars we added, and so many types baked up well. Try things like Reese's Peanut Butter Cups, Snickers bars, Heath bars, and Oreos. If you use Oreos, carefully fold them into the batter, or it will turn a very unappetizing gray color.

make your own flavor
CHEESECAKE

·:· MAKES ONE 12-INCH CHEESECAKE

1 **Make the crust:** Grease a 12-inch springform pan with butter and set aside. In a food processor fitted with the blade attachment, pulse the cookies and sugar until smooth. With the machine running, slowly drizzle in the melted butter and process until combined, about 30 seconds. Press the crumbs into the prepared pan. Wrap the outside of the pan in foil, covering the bottom and halfway up the sides, to prevent any butter in the crust from dripping into the oven.

2 Preheat the oven to 350°F.

3 **Prepare the filling:** In the bowl of a stand mixer fitted with the paddle attachment, beat the cream cheese and sugar on high speed until smooth, 5 minutes.

4 In a medium bowl, whisk the eggs by hand. Add them to the cream cheese mixture. Beat on low speed until combined, 1 minute. Scrape down the sides and around the bottom of the bowl. Beat on high speed for 1 minute. Add the cream, lemon juice, vanilla, and salt. Beat on low speed to combine. Scrape down the sides of the bowl and around the bottom. Beat on high speed until smooth and fluffy, 2 minutes. Using a rubber spatula, fold in the cookies. Pour the filling into the prepared pan, spreading it evenly over the crust. Carefully place the cheesecake into the oven so as not to tear the foil.

5 Bake for 1 hour. Turn off the oven and leave the cheesecake in the oven for another hour. *Do not open the door!*

6 Remove the cheesecake from the oven and let it cool completely. Refrigerate overnight for best results before removing from the pan.

CRUST

½ cup (1 stick) unsalted butter, melted, plus more for the pan

3 cups crushed vanilla wafers (9 ounces)

2 tablespoons sugar

FILLING

4 8-ounce packages cream cheese, at room temperature

1¾ cups sugar

6 large eggs, at room temperature

½ cup heavy whipping cream, at room temperature

2 tablespoons fresh lemon juice

1 tablespoon vanilla extract

¼ teaspoon salt

4 cups coarsely chopped pieces of your favorite cookie or candy bar

I created this recipe in honor of my favorite chef, Michael Symon. One of the biggest thrills of my life was when I got to serve it with him at the South Beach Wine and Food Festival in February 2016! He even featured a clip of us eating this dessert together on ABC's The Chew. *For an even more over-the-top experience, drizzle with Moonshine Caramel Sauce (see Variations, page 121) and sprinkle with Bacon Toffee (page 107) before serving.*

PORK RIND-CRUSTED CHEESECAKE

∴ **MAKES ONE 12 × 18-INCH CHEESECAKE**

1 Preheat the oven to 350°F. Cover a 12 × 18 × 1-inch half-sheet pan with heavy-duty foil. Spray with nonstick cooking spray.

2 **Make the crust:** In a large bowl, crush the pork rinds using your hands. Add the flour, sugar, beaten eggs, bacon grease, and melted butter. Toss all of the ingredients together just until combined. Press the mixture into the prepared pan, pressing it down to make as even a layer as possible.

3 Bake for 15 minutes. Let cool completely.

4 **Prepare the filling:** In a stand mixer fitted with the paddle attachment, beat the cream cheese on high speed until smooth and creamy, 2 minutes. Add the sugar and beat on high speed for 1 minute. Reduce the speed to low and add the eggs, lemon juice, and vanilla. Beat just to combine, then beat on high for 1 minute. Scrape down the sides and around the bottom of the bowl. Beat on high speed for 1 more minute. Spread the mixture evenly over the cooled crust.

5 Bake until the cheesecake is firm and nicely browned, 35 to 40 minutes. Refrigerate overnight for best results.

Nonstick cooking spray

CRUST

1 6-ounce bag original-style pork rinds

½ cup unbleached all-purpose flour

½ cup sugar

2 large eggs, beaten

2 tablespoons bacon grease

2 tablespoons (¼ stick) unsalted butter, melted

FILLING

4 8-ounce packages cream cheese, at room temperature

1 cup (packed) light brown sugar

5 large eggs, at room temperature

1 tablespoon fresh lemon juice

2 tablespoons vanilla extract

COOKIES, bars, and confections

I used to make snickerdoodles with my neighbor who was like my second mother, Joann Seay. I'd climb the fence to go to her house, and, more times than not, I got my clothes caught on the spikes, had to scream for help, got in trouble, and wouldn't get to make cookies that day. Thank goodness that didn't happen every time!

Cookie dough is so versatile—you can make it ahead of time and then roll or cut out shapes with a pretty cookie cutter, scoop it into small balls of dough, or even press it into a half-sheet pan and bake it into bars or a piecrust.

They are practical for parties because they are neat and easy to eat. Cookies can be soft and chewy or crisp and crunchy—I sometimes even use them as a spoon to scoop up ice cream or pudding. Good thing a recipe makes a whole bunch because I can never get enough of them!

I love a classic peanut butter cookie, but sometimes I can't resist adding a little something extra exciting, too. My absolute favorite candy is chocolate peanut butter cups, and I often use them in place of the peanut-and-caramel candy bars in this recipe. It's a delicious way to mix it up a little.

PEANUT BUTTER SURPRISE COOKIES

∴ **MAKES 3 DOZEN 2-INCH COOKIES**

1   Preheat the oven to 350°F. Line two rimmed baking sheets with parchment paper.

2   In a medium bowl, sift together the flour, baking soda, and salt.

3   In the bowl of a stand mixer fitted with the paddle attachment, beat the butter, peanut butter, and both sugars on high speed until light and fluffy, 3 minutes. Scrape down the sides and around the bottom of the bowl. Beat in the eggs and vanilla. Continue beating on high speed for 1 minute. Add the flour mixture and the oats, and beat on low speed just until combined. Add the chopped candy bars and beat for 20 seconds.

4   Drop heaping tablespoons of dough onto the prepared baking sheets 1½ inches apart. There should be 18 cookies per pan. Flatten the dough slightly, making a cross-hatch pattern with the tines of a fork. Freeze the cookies for 10 minutes before baking.

5   Bake until the cookies are golden brown, 10 to 12 minutes. Transfer the pans to a wire rack and let cool. The cookies will keep in an airtight container for 3 to 4 days.

2 cups unbleached all-purpose flour

1 teaspoon baking soda

1 teaspoon salt

1 cup (2 sticks) unsalted butter, at room temperature

1 cup crunchy peanut butter

1 cup granulated sugar

1 cup (packed) dark brown sugar

2 large eggs

2 teaspoons vanilla extract

¼ cup old-fashioned rolled oats

4 1.86-ounce chocolate-covered peanut-and-caramel candy bars (such as Snickers), coarsely chopped

The fresh lemon flavor and the crispness of these cookies is a lovely pairing. They are not too sweet and are especially good crumbled over a bowl of gelato. This recipe is one I picked up during a vacation in Italy. While we were staying at our villa, my friends and I kept a little plate of them on the kitchen counter to enjoy throughout the day. Be sure to plan ahead, since the dough needs to chill for at least 2 hours.

LEMON THINS

MAKES 3 DOZEN 2-INCH COOKIES

2 cups unbleached
all-purpose flour

½ teaspoon ground ginger

½ teaspoon baking soda

¼ teaspoon salt

1 cup sugar

6 tablespoons (¾ stick)
unsalted butter,
at room temperature

1 tablespoon grated lemon
zest

3 tablespoons fresh lemon
juice

1 large egg

1 teaspoon vanilla extract

Nonstick cooking spray

1   In a medium bowl, sift together the flour, ginger, baking soda, and salt.

2   In the bowl of a stand mixer fitted with the paddle attachment, beat the sugar and the butter on high speed until light and fluffy, 5 minutes. Scrape down the sides and around the bottom of the bowl. Add the lemon zest, lemon juice, egg, and vanilla. Beat on high until well blended, 2 minutes. Scrape down the bowl. Beat on high speed for 30 seconds. Add the flour mixture and beat on medium speed until just combined.

3   Turn the dough out onto a large piece of plastic wrap. Press the dough into a disk and refrigerate for 2 hours.

4   Preheat the oven to 400°F. Very lightly spray two rimmed baking sheets with nonstick cooking spray.

5   Using a tablespoon, scoop off pieces of the dough and shape them into balls. Place the dough on the prepared baking sheets 1½ inches apart.

6   Bake until the cookies are set but not hard, 6 to 8 minutes. Remove from the oven and immediately press them with a smooth spatula to flatten out the cookies. Transfer to a wire rack to cool completely. The cookies will keep in an airtight container for 3 to 4 days.

This is a great recipe to make when you want to enlist the help of your little Cookie Monsters (aka kids) and their friends. Once the dough is made, it's just a matter of giving everyone a teaspoon and letting them drop the dough onto the prepared rimmed baking sheets. These cookies have a soft texture with a nice crunch from the rice cereal and are not nearly as sweet as the rice cereal treats made with marshmallow cream. The chocolate and rice cereal make for a good combination. These are perfect for dunking into a cold glass of milk, and they freeze nicely, too.

CHOCOLATE CRUNCH COOKIES

∴ MAKES 6 DOZEN 1-INCH COOKIES

Nonstick cooking spray

2¼ cups unbleached all-purpose flour

1 teaspoon baking soda

½ teaspoon salt

1 cup (2 sticks) unsalted butter, at room temperature

½ cup granulated sugar

½ cup (packed) light brown sugar

2 large eggs

2 teaspoons warm water

1 teaspoon vanilla extract

1 cup crispy rice cereal

1 6-ounce bag mini semisweet chocolate chips

1   Preheat the oven to 375°F. Grease two rimmed baking sheets with nonstick cooking spray.

2   In a medium bowl, sift together the flour, baking soda, and salt.

3   In the bowl of a stand mixer fitted with the paddle attachment, beat the butter and both sugars on high speed until light and fluffy, 3 minutes. Beat in the eggs, warm water, and vanilla on low speed just to blend. Scrape down the sides and around the bottom of the bowl. Beat on high speed for 1 minute. Add the sifted flour mixture. Beat on low speed just until combined. Scrape down the bowl. Beat on high speed for 30 seconds. Using a rubber spatula, gently fold in the cereal and chocolate chips. Working in batches, drop a teaspoon-ful of dough at a time onto the prepared pans, 2 inches apart.

4   Bake until lightly browned, 8 to 10 minutes. Let cool on the pans for 20 minutes. Transfer the cookies to a wire rack to cool completely. The cookies will keep in an airtight container for 3 to 4 days.

I grew up dunking crispy, buttered toast in my coffee—which was really half milk, half coffee, and a whole lot of sugar! Dipping the biscotti into coffee (to soften them up) transports me back to my childhood and the entire "dunking" experience. Never in a million years did I think I would learn to bake these biscotti from an Italian chef while on vacation in Italy using his family recipe! Ain't life grand!

BISCOTTI

⋮ MAKES ABOUT 2 DOZEN BISCOTTI

Nonstick cooking spray

3½ cups unbleached all-purpose flour

1 teaspoon baking powder

¼ teaspoon salt

2 cups plus 2 tablespoons sugar

4 large eggs

2 large egg yolks

Whole milk, as needed

2½ cups coarsely ground almonds

1   Preheat the oven to 325°F. Line a rimmed baking sheet with parchment paper. Lightly coat with nonstick spray.

2   In a medium bowl, sift together the flour, baking powder, and salt.

3   In the bowl of a stand mixer fitted with the paddle attachment, beat the 2 cups sugar, 3 of the eggs, and the egg yolks on high speed until pale yellow, 3 minutes. Add the flour mixture and beat on low speed until just combined. The dough should be smooth but not sticky. Add a little milk (1 or 2 teaspoons), if needed, to get to the right consistency. It is important not to overwork the dough. Fold in the almonds. Let the dough rest for 5 minutes.

4   Divide and shape the dough into 2 loaves that are 4 inches wide and 12 inches long. Beat the remaining egg and brush the loaves with it. Sprinkle the loaves with the remaining 2 tablespoons sugar. Transfer the loaves to the prepared baking sheet.

5   Bake until the surface is crisp and golden, 60 to 65 minutes. Remove from the oven and let cool for 5 minutes on the pan. Using a wide serrated knife, cut the loaves crosswise and on the diagonal into ¾-inch-thick slices. For extra-crispy biscotti, arrange slices cut side up on the pan and bake an additional 10 to 12 minutes. Turn the cookies over and bake on the other side for 10 to 12 minutes. Let cool completely. The cookies will keep in an airtight container for up to 2 weeks.

Variation

CHOCOLATE-DIPPED BISCOTTI   Dip the biscotti into cooled Chocolate Ganache (page 132) and lay them on waxed paper to set. Store in an airtight container.

I love raisins in cakes and cookies, and especially love them in oatmeal raisin cookies. Even though I developed an oatmeal allergy, I didn't want to go the rest of my life without ever eating one of my favorite cookies again, so I came up with this recipe, which excludes the oatmeal but retains all of the soft and yummy goodness that comes from the raisins. The recipe has several variations and makes a gracious plenty (see page 11).

RAISIN COOKIES

∴ **MAKES 6 DOZEN COOKIES**

1   Bring 1 cup water to a boil in a saucepan and add the raisins. Boil for 5 minutes. Remove the pan from the heat and let cool.

2   Preheat the oven to 350°F. Grease two rimmed baking sheets with butter or nonstick cooking spray.

3   In a medium bowl, sift together the flour, baking powder, baking soda, cinnamon (if using), and salt.

4   In the bowl of a stand mixer fitted with the paddle attachment, beat the sugar and melted butter on high speed until light and fluffy, 3 minutes. Add the eggs and vanilla, and beat on high speed for 1 minute. Add the flour mixture, along with the cooled raisins and water. Beat on low speed until combined. Scrape down the sides and around the bottom of the bowl. Increase the speed to high and beat for 1 minute. Using a teaspoon, portion the dough 1½ inches apart onto the prepared pans.

5   Bake until the cookies are browned, 12 to 15 minutes. Let the cookies cool slightly on the pan before using a spatula to transfer them to a wire rack to cool completely. The cookies will keep in an airtight container 3 to 4 days.

Variations

OATMEAL RAISIN COOKIES   For oatmeal raisin cookies, reduce the flour to 3 cups and add 1 cup of old-fashioned oats to the batter.

DRIED CHERRY COOKIES   You could also substitute dried cherries for the dark raisins, or reduce the vanilla to 1 teaspoon and add 1 teaspoon almond extract.

2½ cups dark raisins

1 cup (2 sticks) unsalted butter, melted, plus more for greasing the pan (or use nonstick cooking spray)

4 cups unbleached all-purpose flour

1½ teaspoons baking powder

1 teaspoon baking soda

½ teaspoon ground cinnamon (optional)

½ teaspoon salt

2 cups sugar

3 large eggs

2 teaspoons vanilla extract

I grew up in a wonderful neighborhood where we would play in the creek, ride bikes, play baseball in the summertime, and build snowmen and go sledding in the winter. All the kids were friends, and so were the parents. A few of us still keep in touch, but none as much as Bob and I do. In fact, we live only one block away from each other. I absolutely adore his wife, Jayne, who is quite the baker. Not only does Jayne deliver homemade goodies at Christmas, but she will also happily share the recipe. These rosemary cookies are one of her specialties, and they are perfect in every way!

1 cup (2 sticks) unsalted butter, at room temperature, plus more for greasing the pan (or use nonstick cooking spray)

½ cup granulated sugar

2 cups unbleached all-purpose flour

2 tablespoons rose water

2 teaspoons finely chopped fresh rosemary

Confectioners' sugar, for dusting

ROSEMARY COOKIES

∴ **MAKES 3 DOZEN 1½-INCH COOKIES**

1 Preheat the oven to 275°F. Lightly grease a rimmed baking sheet with butter or nonstick cooking spray.

2 In the bowl of a stand mixer fitted with the paddle attachment, beat the butter and sugar on high speed until light and fluffy, 3 minutes. Add the flour and rose water. Beat on low speed just until combined. Add the rosemary and beat until combined. Using a teaspoon, scoop off pieces of dough, shape them into small balls, and flatten them ever so slightly into ½-inch-thick disks. Place on the prepared pan 1 inch apart.

3 Bake until lightly browned, 15 to 18 minutes. Without opening the door, increase the temperature to 375°F and continue baking for 5 more minutes. Remove from the oven and let cool slightly before dusting with confectioners' sugar while still on the pan. The cookies will keep in an airtight container for 3 to 4 days.

If your tastes lean toward a cookie that's crisp and not too sweet, this one is for you. Pack them in cellophane bags and tie with bakery string for a very pretty teacher gift, especially if you include a handwritten copy of the recipe as the gift tag.

ELEGANT VANILLA WAFERS

·∴· **MAKES 2 DOZEN COOKIES**

¼ cup (½ stick) unsalted butter, at room temperature, plus more for greasing the pan

½ cup sugar

1 large egg

½ teaspoon grated orange zest

1 teaspoon vanilla extract

1 cup unbleached all-purpose flour

1   Preheat the oven to 375°F. Grease a rimmed baking sheet with butter or nonstick cooking spray.

2   In the bowl of a stand mixer fitted with the paddle attachment, beat the butter and sugar on high speed until light and fluffy, 3 minutes. Add the egg, orange zest, and vanilla. Beat on high speed for 30 seconds. Add the flour and beat on low speed just until combined. Drop small spoonfuls of dough onto the prepared pan 2 inches apart.

3   Bake until the edges are browned, 10 to 12 minutes. Let cool completely on the pan. The cookies will keep in an airtight container for 3 to 4 days.

Variation

CHOCOLATE-STRIPED WAFERS   Drizzle the cookies with melted chocolate, then set aside to let the chocolate harden before serving.

When I had my cooking school, Cooking Up a Storm, one of the things my students loved to bake the most was whoopee pies. For fun and giggles, we called them "making whoopee" pies! These are real crowd-pleasers. If you're using the Cream Cheese Frosting, you can make them ahead of time. (I find the whipped cream in the pumpkin filling doesn't hold well if made too far in advance.)

PUMPKIN WHOOPEE PIES

∴ **MAKES 1 DOZEN 4-INCH PIES**

1 Preheat the oven to 350°F. Coat two rimmed baking sheets with Pan Grease (page 16) or shortening with a light dusting of flour. Set aside.

2 In a medium bowl, sift together the flour, baking powder, baking soda, pumpkin pie spice, and salt.

3 In the bowl of a stand mixer fitted with the whisk attachment, beat the oil, eggs, and both sugars on high speed until smooth, 5 minutes. Add the pumpkin and vanilla. Beat on high speed for 30 seconds. Add the flour mixture and beat on low speed just until combined, 30 seconds. Scrape down the sides and around the bottom of the bowl. Beat on high speed for 1 more minute. Using a ¼-cup measure, scoop out the batter onto the prepared baking sheets, making 24 equal-size circles and spacing them about 1 inch apart.

4 Bake until the dough is dome shaped and springs back when touched, 15 to 18 minutes. Transfer the rounds to a wire rack and let cool completely. Turn half of them upside down and spread the flat side with 2 to 3 tablespoons frosting. Top with the remaining pies, flat sides facing. The pies are best eaten the same day they are made.

HINT For a more uniform shape, a muffin top pan works nicely for baking too. The cooking time is the same.

Pan Grease (page 16) or vegetable shortening and extra flour for greasing the pans

3 cups unbleached all-purpose flour

1 teaspoon baking powder

1 teaspoon baking soda

1 teaspoon pumpkin pie spice

1 teaspoon salt

1 cup canola oil

2 large eggs

1 cup granulated sugar

¾ cup (packed) dark brown sugar

3 cups 100% pure pumpkin puree (about 1½ 15-ounce cans)

1 teaspoon vanilla extract

Cream Cheese Frosting (page 123) or ½ recipe Whipped Pumpkin Filling (page 140)

When I was growing up, there was always a box of chocolate-covered cherries on the kitchen counter. Always! They're my mother's favorite candy. It should come as no surprise, then, that this is her favorite cookie, especially when I bake them for her. These cookies also make great ice cream sandwiches; try filling them with either Vanilla (page 202) or Chocolate Ice Cream (page 205).

chocolate cherry
OATMEAL
COOKIES

∴ MAKES 2 DOZEN 3-INCH COOKIES

1 Preheat the oven to 350°F. Line two rimmed baking sheets with parchment paper. Grease the parchment paper with butter.

2 In a medium bowl, sift together the flour, baking soda, and salt.

3 In the bowl of a stand mixer fitted with the paddle attachment, beat the butter and both sugars on high speed until light and fluffy, 3 minutes. Scrape down the sides and around the bottom of the bowl. Add the egg and both extracts, and beat on high speed for 1 minute. Add the flour mixture and beat on low speed just until combined. Beat in the oats, chocolate chips, cherries, and almonds on low speed for 1 more minute. Drop 2 tablespoons of dough onto the prepared pans, 2 inches apart.

4 Bake until golden brown, 8 to 10 minutes. Let the cookies cool on the pans for 15 minutes, then transfer them to a wire rack to cool completely. The cookies will keep in an airtight container for 3 to 4 days.

½ cup (1 stick) unsalted butter, at room temperature, plus more for greasing the pan

1 cup unbleached all-purpose flour

½ teaspoon baking soda

¼ teaspoon salt

½ cup granulated sugar

½ cup (packed) dark brown sugar

1 large egg

½ teaspoon vanilla extract

¼ teaspoon almond extract

¾ cup old-fashioned rolled oats

1½ cups mini semisweet chocolate chips

1 cup dried cherries

½ cup sliced almonds, toasted (see Hint, page 42)

When it comes to making things like cookies, I embrace the "gracious plenty" mentality (page 11) that I grew up with: I like for there to be more than enough when company stops by for a visit. After all, while you're at it, you might as well make enough to feed the masses. These cookies have the perfect consistency. They are soft and crumbly and yet firm but not crunchy. The inside is tender, and their texture makes them perfect for ice cream sandwiches—or to dip into your bowl of ice cream and use as your spoon.

MOCHA CAPPUCCINO COOKIES

MAKES 12 DOZEN 3-INCH COOKIES

2 cups (4 sticks) unsalted butter, at room temperature, plus more for greasing the pans (or use nonstick cooking spray)

5½ cups unbleached all-purpose flour

¾ cup Dutch-processed cocoa powder

¼ cup espresso powder

1 teaspoon baking powder

1 teaspoon baking soda

1 teaspoon salt

4 cups (packed) light brown sugar

4 large eggs

1 12-ounce bag mini semisweet chocolate chips or cinnamon chips

1   Preheat the oven to 350°F. Lightly grease two rimmed baking sheets with butter or nonstick cooking spray.

2   In a medium bowl, sift together the flour, cocoa, espresso powder, baking powder, baking soda, and salt.

3   In the bowl of a stand mixer fitted with the paddle attachment, beat the butter and brown sugar on high speed until light and fluffy, 3 minutes. Scrape down the sides and around the bottom of the bowl. Add the eggs and beat on high speed for 1 minute. Add the flour mixture and beat on low speed just until combined. Beat in the chocolate chips on low speed for 30 seconds. Drop 2 tablespoons of dough onto the prepared pans 1½ inches apart.

4   Bake until set around the edges, 8 to 10 minutes. Let the cookies cool on the pans for 15 minutes, then transfer them to a wire rack to cool completely. The cookies will keep in an airtight container for 3 to 4 days.

I make these delicate little cookies using my mother's cookie press, which she received as a wedding gift back in 1960. A cookie press is a simple tool for making shaped cookies. The dough is put into a cylinder and pushed with a plunger through a metal plate that has a cutout design on it, making cookies into different shapes and sizes. I always double the recipe; 'round my house, we eat these little cookies by the handful, kind of like popcorn. They disappear in a hurry.

CHOCOLATE PILLOWS

·∴· MAKES 5 DOZEN 1½-INCH COOKIES

2¼ cups unbleached all-purpose flour

½ teaspoon salt

1 cup (2 sticks) unsalted butter, at room temperature

¾ cup sugar

1 large egg

2 teaspoons vanilla extract

12 1.55-ounce milk chocolate candy bars (I like Hershey's because they are pre-marked into perfectly shaped rectangles)

Confectioners' sugar, for dusting (optional)

1   Preheat the oven to 375°F. Line a rimmed baking sheet with parchment paper.

2   In a medium bowl, sift the flour and salt.

3   In the bowl of a stand mixer fitted with the paddle attachment, beat the butter and the sugar on high speed until light and fluffy, 3 minutes. Add the egg and vanilla, and beat just to combine. Scrape down the sides and around the bottom of the bowl. Beat on high speed for 1 more minute. Add the flour mixture and beat on low speed just to combine, 1 minute. The flour should be incorporated and the dough smooth.

4   Following the photos on pages 88 and 89, put half of the dough into a cookie press fitted with the sawtooth disk plate. Press the dough onto the prepared pan in 2 ribbon strips. Break each candy bar into 12 rectangular pieces and place each piece lengthwise onto the strips of dough. Put the remaining dough into the cookie press and press the dough on top of the candy, covering it completely. Using a spatula, mark an indentation between the chocolate pieces, being careful not to cut completely through the dough.

5   Bake until the dough is light brown, 10 to 12 minutes. Using a knife, immediately cut through the cookies on the indentations. Let the cookies cool completely on the pan before dusting with confectioners' sugar, if using. Serve at room temperature. The cookies will keep in an airtight container for 2 to 3 days. An extra dusting of confectioners' sugar may be needed before serving.

A visit to Aunt Bobbie's house always meant there would be a plateful of her yummy cookies on the kitchen counter. These crunchy cookies are packed full of finely ground pecans (I like to grind them in a food processor), while the butter and vanilla give them a rich flavor that is made even more delicious with the nice coating of confectioners' sugar. These pretty cookies are perfect for a shower or luncheon dessert. The recipe is easily doubled and the dough freezes nicely, too.

aunt bobbie's
CRESCENT
COOKIES

·∴· **MAKES 4 DOZEN COOKIES**

1 cup (2 sticks) unsalted butter, at room temperature, plus more for greasing the pans (or use nonstick cooking spray)

¾ cup sifted confectioners' sugar, plus more for dusting

2 teaspoons vanilla extract

1 teaspoon ground cinnamon (optional)

1 cup ground pecans

2½ cups sifted unbleached all-purpose flour, plus more for rolling

1 In the bowl of a stand mixer fitted with the paddle attachment, beat the butter and confectioners' sugar on medium-low speed until just combined, increase speed to high, and beat until smooth and creamy, 2 minutes. Add the vanilla, cinnamon (if using), and ground pecans. Beat on low speed just to combine. Scrape down the sides and around the bottom of the bowl. Increase the speed to high and beat for 1 minute. Add the flour and beat on low speed until completely blended. Cover and refrigerate the dough for 2 hours.

2 Preheat the oven to 350°F. Lightly grease two rimmed baking sheets with butter or nonstick cooking spray.

3 With lightly floured hands, pinch off about 2 heaping teaspoons of dough, roll it into a log, then bend the dough slightly to form a crescent shape. Each one should be about 4 inches long and ¾ inch in diameter. Repeat with the remaining dough and put them on the prepared baking sheet 1 to 1½ inches apart.

4 Bake until lightly browned on the bottom, about 15 minutes. While still warm, roll the cookies in confectioners' sugar for the best coverage. Let cool completely on a wire rack with parchment or wax paper underneath to catch the confectioners' sugar that comes off the cookies. You can sprinkle it back over the cookies once they are in a container.

5 The cookies will keep in an airtight container for 3 to 4 days. If the cookies last longer than a day or two, they will need more confectioners' sugar sifted over them, as it tends to dissolve into the moist cookie.

Variation

CHOCOLATE-DIPPED CRESCENTS Omit the confectioners'
sugar and drizzle these cookies with Chocolate Ganache (page
132), or dip the ends into the ganache first and then into finely
chopped pecans.

Divinity, a light and delicate egg white, sugar, and pecan confection cut into bits, is about as authentic Southern as you can get (except for tomato aspic, which is another recipe for another book). When it comes to baking, what's going on outside definitely plays a role in how things turn out inside your kitchen. It's true what they say about the weather and the humidity, and it applies to this candy, too. Maybe that's why, here in the South, divinity is a holiday treat, since the colder, less humid weather helps it turn out just right.

3 cups sugar

¾ cup light corn syrup

¼ teaspoon baking soda

½ teaspoon vanilla extract

3 large egg whites

1½ cups finely chopped pecans

DIVINITY

∴ **MAKES 4 DOZEN PIECES**

1 Line two 12 × 18 × 1-inch half-sheet pans with parchment paper.

2 In a medium saucepan set over low heat, dissolve the sugar, corn syrup, and baking soda in ¾ cup of water. Bring to a low boil and cook, without stirring, until a candy thermometer reaches 248°F, the firm-ball stage, 15 to 20 minutes. The liquid in the middle of the saucepan will look like it's spinning a thread. Remove the pan from the heat and stir in the vanilla.

3 In the bowl of a stand mixer fitted with the whisk attachment, beat the egg whites on high speed until stiff, about 5 minutes. With the mixer running on high speed, pour in the syrup mixture in a slow and steady stream, taking 8 to 10 minutes to incorporate it. Continue beating until the mixture holds its shape, 2 minutes. Decrease the speed to medium, add the pecans, and beat just until the pecans are incorporated.

4 Use a tablespoon to scoop the candy and another spoon to scrape the candy from the spoon and drop it onto the parchment paper. Repeat with the remaining candy and cool completely before serving. Divinity is best enjoyed within a day or two of being made.

This recipe is by far the most versatile one in the book. It makes an abundance of cookies and ornaments, a fabulous piecrust (or ice cream pie, page 96), and a delicious ice cream sandwich with Eggnog Ice Cream (page 212). More than anything, this recipe holds a very special place in my heart for all the wonderful memories it brings up, since I've baked these cookies for many a performance of Ballet Spartanburg's The Nutcracker.

GINGERBREAD COOKIES

·∴· MAKES A GENEROUS 3 DOZEN 3-INCH COOKIES
    OR ORNAMENTS

Nonstick cooking spray

7 cups unbleached all-purpose flour, plus more for rolling

2 teaspoons baking soda

1 teaspoon ground allspice

1 teaspoon ground ginger

1 teaspoon ground cloves

1 teaspoon ground cinnamon

1 teaspoon salt

⅓ cup vegetable shortening

1 cup (packed) light or dark brown sugar

1½ cups molasses

⅔ cup ice water

1   Preheat the oven to 350°F. Lightly grease two rimmed baking sheets with nonstick cooking spray.

2   In a medium bowl, sift together the flour, baking soda, allspice, ginger, cloves, cinnamon, and salt.

3   In the large bowl of a stand mixer fitted with the paddle attachment, beat the shortening, brown sugar, and molasses on high speed until combined, 1 minute. Add the ice water. Add the flour mixture and beat on low speed just to combine. Increase the speed to high and beat until the dough pulls away from the sides of the bowl, about 2 minutes.

4   Separate the dough into 4 equal portions. Working with one at a time on a floured work surface, roll the dough out until it is ⅜ inch thick. Cut out gingerbread man shapes and place them on the prepared pans. Repeat with the remaining dough.

5   Bake until set around the edges and slightly puffy, 10 to 12 minutes. Do not overbake or the cookies will be too hard to enjoy. Cool slightly before moving the cookies to a wire rack to cool completely. The cookies will keep in an airtight container up to 4 days. These cookies are great for decorating, too.

HINT   If this recipe makes too much for your mixer to handle, cut it in half.

recipe continues

Variations

FOR ORNAMENTS   Use a drinking straw to cut a hole in the top of each cookie (for threading a ribbon to hang the gingerbread) and then bake at 250°F for 1 hour.

FOR PIECRUST   Lightly coat an 11-inch tart pan with a removable bottom with nonstick spray. Roll 2 cups of dough very thin (it will rise during baking) and press it into the bottom and up the sides of the prepared pan. Using your fingers, break away the excess dough at the top edge. Bake at 350°F until the crust has risen slightly, 12 to 14 minutes. Let cool completely or even freeze before filling with Eggnog Custard (page 211), Eggnog Ice Cream (see Variations, page 212), or Lemon Curd Ice Cream (page 201).

If you're searching for the perfect dessert for your summertime party, look no further. Make and cut these ahead of time, and store them in the freezer. All that's left to do after that is decide if you want to add a little Vanilla Buttercream Frosting (page 126) and toasted coconut (see Hint, page 177) to your cookies, make them into ice cream sandwiches with Rum Raisin Ice Cream (page 203), or simply serve them cut into bars.

PINEAPPLE BARS

∴ **MAKES 28 BARS OR 56 TRIANGLES**

1 Preheat the oven to 350°F. Line a 12 × 18 × 1-inch rimmed baking sheet with a long sheet of foil, letting the short edges hang over the sides, and coat the foil with Pan Grease (page 16) or butter or shortening.

2 In a medium bowl, sift together the flour, baking powder, baking soda, and salt.

3 In the bowl of a stand mixer fitted with the paddle attachment, beat the butter, shortening, and both sugars on high speed until light and fluffy, about 3 minutes. Beat in the eggs, pineapple, and vanilla. Scrape down the sides and around the bottom of the bowl. Beat on high speed for 1 more minute. Add the flour mixture and nuts, and beat just to combine. Scrape down the bowl. Beat on high speed for 30 seconds. Press the dough evenly into the bottom of the prepared pan, but not up the sides.

4 Bake until golden brown, 18 to 20 minutes. Let cool completely before using the foil overhang to lift the bars out of the pan. Mark the long side to get 7 columns. Mark the short side to get 4 rows. You will get 28 bars or, if you halve them on the diagonal, 56 smaller triangles.

Variations

ICE CREAM SANDWICHES A muffin-top pan with twelve 3-inch cups can also be used to make round cookies, perfect for ice cream sandwiches. This recipe will make 24 cookies for 12 ice cream sandwiches. The cooking time for baking round cookies is the same.

ICE CREAM "GRACIOUS PLENTY" PIE If you're too busy to assemble individual ice cream sandwiches, spread 8 cups of ice cream over the cold uncut dough and make an ice cream "gracious plenty" pie instead.

Pan Grease (page 16) or butter or shortening

4 cups unbleached all-purpose flour

2 teaspoons baking powder

½ teaspoon baking soda

½ teaspoon salt

½ cup (1 stick) unsalted butter, at room temperature

½ cup vegetable shortening

1¼ cups granulated sugar

¾ cup (packed) light brown sugar

2 large eggs

1 cup crushed pineapple, well drained

1 teaspoon vanilla extract

1 cup finely chopped macadamia nuts

I have never been to a party where lemon squares weren't on the dessert table. This is a simple recipe, but don't let that fool you. These are light and delicious, and they can be made ahead of time.

LEMON SQUARES

∴ MAKES 4½ DOZEN 2-INCH SQUARES

1 Preheat the oven to 350°F. Line a 12 × 18 × 1-inch half-sheet pan with foil, allowing it to hang over the two short sides so it's easy to lift out the squares. Lightly coat the foil with nonstick cooking spray.

2 **Make the crust:** In a food processor fitted with the blade attachment, blend together the flour, confectioners' sugar, and salt. With the processor running, add the butter, a few pieces at a time, until the mixture comes together. Press the dough into the bottom of the prepared pan and refrigerate uncovered for 30 minutes.

3 Bake the crust until lightly browned, 15 to 18 minutes.

4 **Meanwhile, prepare the filling:** In the bowl of a stand mixer fitted with the whisk attachment, beat the eggs, sugar, lemon zest, lemon juice, flour, and salt on low speed until smooth, 2 minutes. Increase the speed to high and beat for 1 minute.

5 Pour the filling over the baked crust. Bake until the filling is set, 25 to 30 minutes. Let cool completely before dusting with confectioners' sugar.

6 Carefully lift the foil from the pan and place the pastry on a flat surface. Mark the long and short side every 2 inches to get nine columns and six rows (you should get about 54 squares). The squares will keep in an airtight container in the refrigerator for 3 to 4 days. You will probably need to dust with additional confectioner's sugar, as it will get absorbed into the moist custard.

Variation

ORANGE SQUARES Reduce the granulated sugar to 1½ cups. Substitute 3 tablespoons fresh orange zest and ½ cup orange juice for the lemon zest and juice. For an adult version, add ¼ cup Grand Marnier. You can also brush a little Grand Marnier over the cooled squares before dusting with the confectioners' sugar.

Nonstick cooking spray

CRUST

2 cups unbleached all-purpose flour

¾ cup confectioners' sugar

½ teaspoon salt

1 cup (2 sticks) unsalted butter, cut into small cubes, at room temperature

FILLING

6 large eggs

2½ cups granulated sugar

3 tablespoons grated lemon zest

¾ cup fresh lemon juice

⅔ cup unbleached all-purpose flour

½ teaspoon salt

Confectioners' sugar, for dusting

There was a candy bar in Ireland I fell in love with called a Dime bar (also known as a Daim bar) that's like the Heath bar here in the United States. While eating my way through Ireland on my "bakery babes" tour, I enjoyed a few of the beloved Dime bars—along with a pint or two—every day! This candy bar has the perfect combination of chocolate on the outside and buttery toffee on the inside, with just the right amount of crunch. It's the bits of candy bar that make these cookies some of the best you will ever put in your mouth. I can honestly say I have made thousands of them over the years, and they always receive rave reviews!

BUTTER BRICKLE COOKIES

∴ **MAKES 1½ DOZEN 3-INCH COOKIES**

1 cup (2 sticks) unsalted butter, plus more for the pan (or use nonstick cooking spray)

3½ cups unbleached all-purpose flour

1 teaspoon baking soda

1 teaspoon salt

1 8-ounce bag chocolate-covered toffee bits (I like Heath English Toffee Bits)

3 tablespoons canola oil

¾ cup granulated sugar

¾ cup (packed) light brown sugar

1 teaspoon vanilla extract

2 large eggs

1   Preheat the oven to 325°F. Grease a rimmed baking sheet with butter or nonstick cooking spray.

2   In a medium bowl, sift together 2¾ cups of the flour, the baking soda, and salt.

3   In a separate medium bowl, toss together the toffee bits, oil, and the remaining ¾ cup flour.

4   In the bowl of a stand mixer fitted with the paddle attachment, beat the butter, both sugars, and vanilla on high speed until light and fluffy, 3 minutes. Scrape down the sides and around the bottom of the bowl. Add the eggs and beat on high speed for 1 minute. Add the flour mixture and beat on low speed just until combined. Add the toffee mixture and beat on low speed just until combined. Drop 2 tablespoons of dough onto the prepared pan, 1½ inches apart.

5   Bake until lightly browned, 10 to 12 minutes. Let cool slightly before moving the cookies to a wire rack to cool completely. The cookies will keep in an airtight container for 3 to 4 days.

Sweet and bite-sized, these cookies are perfect for a bridal or baby shower, especially when arranged on a tiered dessert stand. Browning the butter adds a wonderful nutty aroma and flavor. Even though they are dainty little bites, these cookies are rich and decadent.

BROWN BUTTER PECAN BITES

⋮ MAKES 3 DOZEN 2-INCH COOKIES

1   Preheat the oven to 350°F. Lightly grease a rimmed baking sheet using nonstick cooking spray.

2   In the bowl of a stand mixer fitted with the paddle attachment, beat the butter and both sugars on high speed until light and fluffy, 3 minutes. Add the egg yolk and vanilla, and beat on low speed to combine. Scrape down the sides and around the bottom of the bowl. Beat on high speed for 1 minute. Add the flour and beat on low speed just to combine. Scrape down the bowl. Beat on high speed until the dough is stiff, 1 minute.

3   Using a tablespoon, scoop off pieces of the dough and shape them into balls with wet hands to keep the dough from sticking. Place the balls on the prepared pan and flatten with the palm of your hand. Sprinkle each with a pinch of granulated sugar.

4   Bake until the cookies are golden brown, 8 to 10 minutes. Let cool completely. Frost the cookies and press a pecan half into the top of each one. The cookies are best enjoyed at room temperature but can be stored in an airtight container in the refrigerator.

Nonstick cooking spray

¾ cup (1½ sticks) unsalted butter, at room temperature

½ cup (packed) light brown sugar

1 tablespoon granulated sugar, plus more for sprinkling

1 large egg yolk

1 teaspoon vanilla extract

2 cups sifted unbleached all-purpose flour

Browned Butter Frosting (recipe follows)

24 pecan halves, toasted (see Hint, page 42)

BROWNED BUTTER FROSTING

·∴· MAKES 2 CUPS

½ cup (1 stick) unsalted butter

3 cups sifted confectioners' sugar

1 teaspoon vanilla extract

2 to 4 tablespoons heavy whipping cream

1   In a large heavy-bottomed stainless-steel skillet set over medium heat, melt the butter. (You'll want to use a stainless skillet so that you can see the butter as it starts to brown; it can go from brown to black in a hurry.) Cook, whisking constantly as the butter first foams and then subsides, until it smells nutty, 8 to 10 minutes. Watch it carefully so that it doesn't burn.

2   Remove the pan from the heat. Whisk in the confectioners' sugar and vanilla until blended. Slowly whisk in the whipping cream until the frosting has a spreadable consistency, being careful not to make it too thin (you may not use all of the whipping cream).

Meringues can be finicky, but don't let that intimidate you. I don't recommend baking these cookies on a real humid or rainy day; instead, wait for the weather to cooperate. It's worth it. You'll be glad you did.

ALMOND MERINGUES

·∴· **MAKES 3 DOZEN COOKIES**

4 large egg whites, at room temperature

¼ teaspoon cream of tartar

1 teaspoon vanilla extract

1 cup sugar

½ cup almonds, toasted (see Hint, page 42) and finely chopped

½ cup hazelnuts, toasted (see Hint, page 42) and finely chopped

1 Preheat the oven to 300°F. Line two rimmed baking sheets with parchment paper.

2 Using a stand mixer with the whisk attachment, beat the egg whites, cream of tartar, and vanilla on high speed until soft peaks form, 2 minutes. With the mixer running, gradually add the sugar in a slow stream and continue beating on high speed until stiff peaks form, about 5 minutes. Using a rubber spatula, gently fold in the nuts. Drop the batter by heaping tablespoonfuls onto the prepared baking sheets 1 inch apart.

3 Bake until the cookies turn slightly golden and are crisp mounds, 25 to 30 minutes. Immediately transfer to a wire rack to prevent the meringues from sticking. Let cool completely. The cookies will keep in an airtight container for 1 to 2 days.

These bars are more like a brownie and are perfectly delicious without any frosting, though I usually like to gild the lily. If you want to really get the party started, brush the cooled cake with some good-quality bourbon before frosting it and cutting it into bars.

PUMPKIN BARS

∴ **MAKES 2½ DOZEN BARS**

1 Preheat the oven to 350°F. Coat an 11 × 15 × 2-inch jelly roll pan with Pan Grease (page 16) or butter with a light dusting of flour.

2 In a medium bowl, sift together the flour, baking soda, salt, and pumpkin pie spice.

3 In the bowl of a stand mixer fitted with the whisk attachment, beat the sugar, oil, eggs, and pumpkin on medium speed until smooth and creamy, 2 minutes. Increase to the speed to high and beat for 1 minute. Add the flour mixture and beat on low speed just to combine. Increase the speed to high and beat for 1 minute. Using a rubber spatula, fold in the pecans. Pour the batter into the prepared pan and spread evenly to smooth the top.

4 Bake until the center springs back when lightly touched, 28 to 30 minutes. Let cool completely before frosting and cutting into squares. The bars will keep in an airtight container for 3 to 4 days without frosting; if you frost them, it's best to keep them in the refrigerator for 3 to 4 days.

HINT One of the best things about bar cookies, or any dessert baked in a sheet pan really, is that they can be cut into the size that works for the occasion. You can cut them into 2-bite pieces for a cookie-snack, or into larger bars for a plated dessert that will allow room for some fresh whipped cream or even a scoop of ice cream on top.

Pan Grease (page 16) or butter or shortening and extra flour for the pan

2 cups unbleached all-purpose flour

1 teaspoon baking soda

½ teaspoon salt

1½ teaspoons pumpkin pie spice

2 cups sugar

1 cup canola oil

4 large eggs

1 15-ounce can 100% pure pumpkin puree

1 cup coarsely chopped pecans, toasted (see Hint, page 42)

Cream Cheese Frosting (page 123), optional

I created this recipe to go along with the Pork Rind–Crusted Cheesecake (page 69) that I made for chef Michael Symon. It's perfect for crumbling over the cheesecake with a drizzle of Moonshine Caramel Sauce (see Variations, page 121), or to enjoy it all by itself.

BACON TOFFEE

⸫ **MAKES 3 POUNDS, OR ONE 12 × 18 × 1-INCH HALF-SHEET PAN**

2 pounds thin-sliced bacon

2 cups (4 sticks) unsalted butter

½ teaspoon salt

3 scant cups sugar

12 1.55-ounce milk chocolate bars (I like Hershey's)

1   Preheat the oven to 400°F.

2   Arrange the bacon on two 12 × 18-inch rimmed baking sheets, putting 1 pound on each pan. Roast until crispy, about 15 minutes. Transfer the bacon to paper towels to drain. Once cool, chop it finely. Wipe one of the sheet pans lightly with a paper towel (leave 1 to 2 tablespoons of baking grease behind). Spread the finely chopped bacon evenly over the pan.

3   In a 4-quart heavy-bottomed saucepan set over medium heat, melt the butter. Add the salt and sugar and stir just to combine. Without stirring, let the mixture bubble and thicken for 25 to 30 minutes. The mixture will become a medium caramel color. Pour the hot caramel directly onto the diced bacon, making sure the bacon stays evenly distributed on the pan, and spread it evenly with an offset spatula. Immediately top the toffee with the chocolate bars. Allow the chocolate bars to melt for 5 minutes before spreading evenly over the toffee. I prefer to use an offset spatula for spreading the melted candy bars.

4   Let cool completely. It is best to refrigerate the toffee overnight. Break the cooled toffee into small pieces to serve (I use an ice pick). Store the toffee in the refrigerator for up to a week or freeze.

My mother's favorite candy is chocolate-covered cherries, and she loves making her own special batch. What's so great about this recipe is you can very easily double or even triple it and have plenty of cherries for everyone! Be sure you set aside a little extra time if you're making more than a 16-ounce jar. It can take a while, but what a treat!

CHOCOLATE- COVERED CHERRIES

·:· **MAKES 30 CHOCOLATE-COVERED CHERRIES**

30 maraschino cherries with stems, blotted dry, plus 2 tablespoons reserved cherry juice

¼ cup (½ stick) unsalted butter, at room temperature

3 cups confectioners' sugar, sifted

Good pinch of salt

1 pound white, milk, or dark melting chocolate

1   Freeze the cherries on a waxed paper–lined rimmed baking sheet for 1 hour.

2   In the bowl of a stand mixer fitted with the whisk attachment, beat the butter on high speed until smooth, 1 minute. Reduce the speed to low and, while running, slowly add 2 cups of the confectioners' sugar and the salt. Add 1 tablespoon of cherry juice and beat on low speed while adding the last cup of confectioners' sugar. Add 1 more tablespoon of cherry juice. The mixture should be stiff. Put the dough on a piece of plastic wrap and flatten it into a disk. Refrigerate for 1 to 2 hours.

3   Unwrap the dough. Using a melon baller or a teaspoon, measure out 30 cherry-sized dough balls.

4   Remove the cherries from the freezer. Press each dough ball into a flat disk big enough to cover each cherry, and wrap the cherries. Freeze for 1 hour.

5   In a metal bowl set over a pan of simmering water or in a double boiler, stir the chocolate as it melts and becomes smooth. Make sure the bottom of the bowl doesn't touch the water. Remove the pan from the heat. While holding the stem and using a fork to balance the cherry, carefully dip each cherry into the chocolate. Place each chocolate-covered cherry onto a sheet of wax paper to set. (If desired, give them a second dip in the chocolate.)

6   Refrigerate the cherries until the chocolate is firm, 1 hour. The cherries will keep in an airtight container in the refrigerator for up to a month.

Variation

LIQUEUR-SOAKED CHERRIES Soak
the drained cherries in moonshine or
your favorite liqueur for a week before
wrapping them in the sugar dough and
dipping them in chocolate.

Even though these pecan balls are nothing fancy, they are really good and fun to make. They are also great as a hostess gift around the holidays and stack nicely in a decorative tin.

PECAN BALLS

∴ **MAKES 4 DOZEN COOKIES**

2½ cups small/broken pieces vanilla wafers

2 tablespoons Dutch-processed cocoa powder

1 cup confectioners' sugar, plus more for rolling

1 cup ground pecans

⅓ cup dark rum

3 tablespoons light corn syrup

1   In the bowl of a food processor fitted with the blade attachment, pulse together the vanilla wafer pieces, cocoa, and confectioners' sugar.

2   In a large bowl, combine the ground pecans, rum, and corn syrup. Add the vanilla wafer mixture and stir until the mixture holds together and forms a dough. Using a tablespoon, scoop off pieces of the dough, shape them into 1-inch balls, and roll in confectioners' sugar.

3   The pecan balls will keep in an airtight container for 5 days and might need to be dusted with additional confectioners' sugar before serving.

If you're looking for a quick and easy treat, this one's for you! With just three ingredients and only two pans to wash, why not keep this chocolate bark around all the time?

CHOCOLATE PEANUT BUTTER BARK

∴ **MAKES 2¾ POUNDS (AKA A GRACIOUS PLENTY!)**

1 12-ounce bag best-quality white chocolate chips

1 cup crunchy peanut butter

1 12-ounce bag best-quality semisweet chocolate chips

Chopped roasted peanuts, for sprinkling on top

1 Line a rimmed baking sheet with parchment paper.

2 In a metal bowl set over a pan of simmering water or in a double boiler, melt the white chocolate chips and peanut butter, stirring until smooth. Make sure the bottom of the bowl doesn't touch the water. Pour the mixture into the prepared pan, spreading it evenly to the edges and into the corners.

3 In a clean metal bowl set over a pan of simmering water or in a double boiler, melt the semisweet chocolate chips, stirring until smooth. Again, make sure the bottom of the bowl doesn't touch the water. Pour the dark chocolate over the white chocolate and peanut butter mixture and, using the back of a tablespoon, swirl the mixtures together to give them a marbled look. Sprinkle with the chopped peanuts.

4 Refrigerate, uncovered, until firm. Break the bark into pieces to serve. The bark will keep in an airtight container at room temperature for 1 week, or freeze it to enjoy later.

Variation

CHOCOLATE ALMOND BUTTER BARK Almond butter can be used in place of the peanut butter. Toasted sliced almonds (page 42) are pretty sprinkled on top.

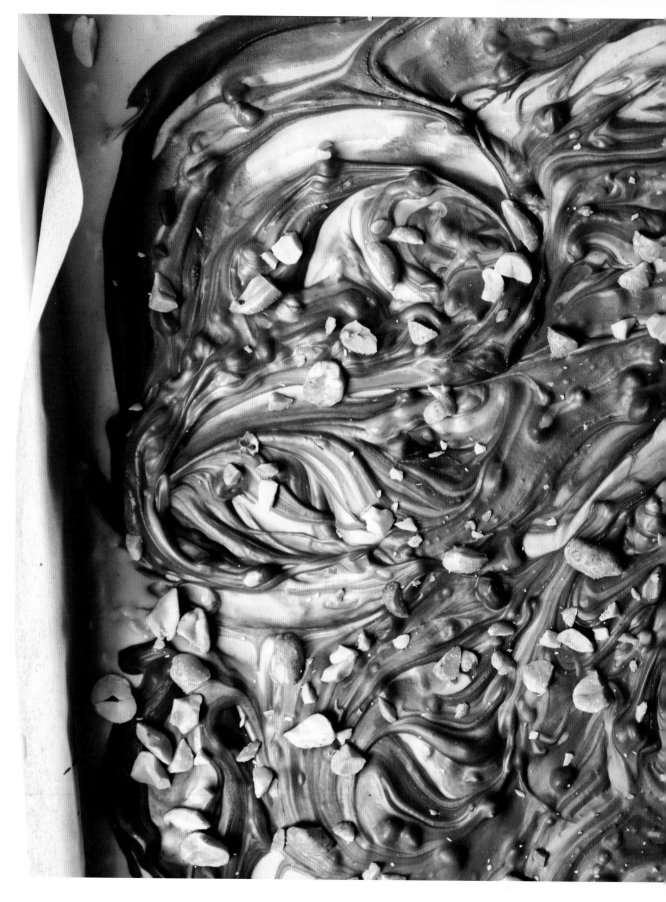

FROSTINGS, fillings, and sauces

I've had my share of disasters in the kitchen! I've burned pies, scorched puddings, blown the lid off a blender while trying to puree a steaming fruit filling, and even melted a few plastic bowls by placing them on a hot burner. There was absolutely nothing I could do to salvage these mistakes. Thank goodness for a big, sturdy trash bag!

However, if the mistake is repairable and your cake layers only come out uneven or a little dry, just get those creative juices flowing and don't worry. There's nothing like a good frosting, filling, or sauce to cover that little mistake right up and make your dessert perfectly delicious. No one will be the wiser.

Even if you're not trying to cover up a baking mishap, the simplest, most basic cake can be made into a showstopping dessert with delicious frosting, filling, or sauce between the layers, over the outside layers, or even down in the hole of a pound cake. Create your signature dessert by mixing things up a little and adding your own flair. Variety is the spice of life!

This is it! This is the chocolate frosting recipe that went on the yellow cake that was the very first cake my mother and I baked and sold. Back when I taught cooking classes, we used bacon in at least one recipe every week, and anytime my mother had some of this leftover frosting in the fridge, one of my students would always dip her crunchy bacon in a little bowl of it. Whenever I see Suzan we always laugh about how much bacon and chocolate frosting she ate every week!

1 cup (2 sticks) unsalted butter, at room temperature

2 16-ounce boxes confectioners' sugar, sifted

¼ to ½ cup evaporated milk

1 cup Dutch-processed cocoa powder

2 teaspoons vanilla extract

CHOCOLATE FROSTING

⠿ **MAKES ENOUGH FOR ONE 9-INCH 4-LAYER CAKE OR 24 CUPCAKES**

1 In the bowl of a stand mixer fitted with the paddle attachment, beat the butter on high speed until smooth, 1 minute. Scrape down the sides and around the bottom of the bowl. With the mixer on low speed, gradually add half of the confectioners' sugar and 2 tablespoons of the evaporated milk. Gradually add the remaining box of confectioners' sugar, the cocoa, and vanilla. Scrape down the bowl. With the mixer still on low speed, add 2 more tablespoons of the evaporated milk. Increase the speed to high and beat until light and fluffy, 1 minute. If the frosting is still too thick to spread, beat in more evaporated milk, 1 tablespoon at a time, on low speed. Be careful not to make the frosting too thin, or it won't stay on the sides of the cake.

2 The frosting will keep in an airtight container in the refrigerator for up to 2 weeks.

Variation

MOCHA FROSTING Dissolve 2 tablespoons espresso powder in the evaporated milk before adding it to the confectioners' sugar.

Few things are any better than a rich and creamy caramel sauce, unless that caramel sauce is going into a buttercream frosting. This frosting works well on yellow layer cake (page 21) or carrot cake (page 39). If you have extra caramel sauce in the house, add a drizzle of that, too.

2 cups (4 sticks) unsalted butter, at room temperature

1 16-ounce box confectioners' sugar

1 teaspoon vanilla extract

1 recipe Caramel Sauce (recipe follows)

CARAMEL FROSTING

∴ **MAKES ENOUGH FOR ONE 9-INCH 4-LAYER CAKE OR 24 CUPCAKES**

1   In the bowl of a stand mixer fitted with the paddle attachment, beat the butter, confectioners' sugar, and vanilla on low speed until smooth, 2 minutes. Scrape down the sides and around the bottom of the bowl. Gradually increase the speed to high. With the mixer running, pour in 1 cup of the cooled caramel sauce in a slow and steady stream, reserving the remaining ½ cup to drizzle over the frosting between the cake layers.

2   Refrigerate the frosting for 1 to 2 hours before using.

recipe continues

This caramel sauce is especially marvelous over ice cream, drizzled over pound cake (page 31), or even right out of the jar on a spoon.

1½ cups granulated sugar

¼ teaspoon baking soda

1 cup heavy cream

CARAMEL SAUCE

·∴· MAKES 1½ CUPS

1   In a 2-quart heavy-bottomed saucepan set over medium-high heat, whisk together the sugar, baking soda, and ¼ cup water. Bring the mixture to a gentle boil. Reduce the heat to medium and cook, whisking around the sides of the pan to fully combine the ingredients. Without any further whisking, let the sauce cook until it becomes deep amber in color, 12 to 15 minutes.

2   Remove the pan from the heat and add the cream very slowly and carefully to prevent the sauce from bubbling up and out of the pan, causing a splash and a possible burn. Whisk constantly until smooth and let cool completely, 4 hours or overnight.

Variations

SALTED CARAMEL SAUCE   Add 1 teaspoon kosher salt to the caramel sauce after whisking in the heavy cream.

MOONSHINE CARAMEL SAUCE   For serving with the Pork Rind—Crusted Cheesecake (page 69), add 1 to 2 tablespoons moonshine (or bourbon) after letting the sauce cool for 30 to 45 minutes. The sauce needs to cool so the heat doesn't cause the alcohol to cook out.

This is Daisy Cakes' signature frosting. It's simply delicious. There are countless things you can add to it—like zest, nuts, curd, and even bacon—to really dress it up and make it your own signature frosting. Let your imagination run wild!

1 cup (2 sticks) unsalted butter, at room temperature

2 8-ounce packages cream cheese, cold

2 teaspoons vanilla extract

2 16-ounce boxes confectioners' sugar, sifted

CREAM CHEESE FROSTING

∴ **MAKES ENOUGH FOR ONE 9-INCH 4-LAYER CAKE OR 24 CUPCAKES**

1 In the bowl of a stand mixer fitted with the paddle attachment, beat the butter on medium speed until smooth, 1 minute. Scrape down the sides and around the bottom of the bowl. Add the cream cheese and vanilla and beat on high speed until smooth, 1 minute.

2 With the mixer on low speed, gradually add the confectioners' sugar just until blended. Scrape down the bowl. Increase the speed to high and beat until smooth and fluffy, about 1 minute. The frosting will keep in an airtight container in the refrigerator for 7 to 10 days.

Variations

FLAVORED CREAM CHEESE FROSTING Reduce the vanilla to 1 teaspoon and add 1 teaspoon of your favorite extract to accompany your cake layers. Butterscotch extract is a delicious addition to the frosting for the Carrot Cake (page 39), and almond extract is perfect for Miss Geraldine's Italian Cream Cake (page 35).

MOONSHINE CREAM CHEESE FROSTING For an adult version, add 2 tablespoons of your favorite moonshine or bourbon along with 1 teaspoon vanilla extract.

LEMON CREAM CHEESE FROSTING For a fresh take on lemon frosting, add 1 teaspoon lemon extract along with 2 tablespoons grated fresh lemon zest. Equal amounts of orange zest and extract are delicious, too.

BACON CREAM CHEESE FROSTING If you're a sweet and salty fan, add ½ pound finely chopped crispy bacon, making sure the bacon is cooled and very well drained before adding.

This filling is delicious spread on top of Cream Cheese Frosting (page 123) or in between yellow cake layers (page 21). It's also perfect mixed right into the frosting. I love using it as a fun surprise inside a Carrot Cake cupcake (page 39)—simply scoop out a teaspoon of the cake and fill the hole with some of this bacon jam before frosting.

BACON JAM
FILLING with bourbon

⋰ MAKES 2 CUPS

1½ pounds applewood smoked bacon, chopped

3 cups chopped sweet onions (2 large)

⅓ cup good-quality bourbon

¼ cup balsamic vinegar

½ cup (packed) dark brown sugar

½ to 1 teaspoon freshly ground black pepper, to taste

1 In a large heavy-bottomed pot set over medium heat, cook the chopped bacon until crispy, 10 to 12 minutes. (Once the bacon is about halfway browned and has rendered fat, I like to prop the handle of the pot on top of a box of kosher salt—or something else about that height—to create a "deep end" of the pot, so that the bacon can cook better in its rendered fat and not burn the bottom of the pan. If you try this trick, make sure the pot—and box—are sturdy so neither tips over). Using a slotted spoon, transfer the bacon to paper towels to cool and drain.

2 Pour off all but ¼ cup of the bacon grease. Add the onions and cook over medium-low heat, stirring occasionally, until caramelized, 20 to 25 minutes.

3 While the onions are cooking, combine the bourbon and vinegar in a glass measuring cup. When the onions are caramelized, add the bourbon mixture. Scrape up the browned bits from the bottom of the pan as the liquid bubbles away. Stir in the brown sugar and pepper. Add the bacon, reduce the heat to low, and cook until the mixture develops a jam-like consistency. If the mixture becomes too thick or starts to stick to the bottom of the pot, add a little water; ¼ to ½ cup should be enough. Let cool completely. The jam will keep in an airtight container in the refrigerator for up to 1 month.

When I was growing up, there was a local bakery where everybody bought birthday party cakes. The cakes were very pretty, but the frosting tasted funny and was a little bit greasy. It wasn't until I started Daisy Cakes that I came to understand not all buttercream frostings are created equal. A true buttercream is made with butter, not *vegetable shortening. Try this one and taste the difference.*

2 cups (4 sticks) unsalted butter, at room temperature

6 cups confectioners' sugar, sifted (a little less than 2 1-pound boxes)

¼ cup heavy whipping cream, plus more if needed

1 tablespoon vanilla extract

VANILLA BUTTERCREAM FROSTING

MAKES ENOUGH FOR ONE 9-INCH 4-LAYER CAKE OR 2 DOZEN CUPCAKES

In the bowl of a stand mixer fitted with the paddle attachment, beat the butter on high speed until smooth, 1 minute. Scrape down the sides and around the bottom of the bowl. With the mixer on low speed, gradually add 3 cups of the confectioners' sugar and 2 tablespoons of the cream, and beat for 1 minute. Scrape down the bowl. Gradually add the remaining confectioners' sugar, cream, and the vanilla. Beat on high speed for 1 minute. If the frosting needs to be thinner, add more cream, 1 tablespoon at a time, and beat on high speed for 1 minute. The frosting will keep in an airtight container in the refrigerator for up to 2 weeks.

Variation

PEPPERMINT FROSTING   For a pretty cake for St. Patrick's Day, add ½ cup white chocolate ganache (page 132) to the frosting, along with 1 teaspoon peppermint extract (omitting the vanilla extract) and 1 to 2 drops of green food coloring.

At both of my grandmothers' houses, there was always a covered candy dish with two kinds of hard candy in it: peppermint and butterscotch. The creamy butterscotch in the pretty yellow wrapper was always my favorite. This frosting makes me think of that smooth, buttery candy. Be sure to give the brown sugar and whipping cream a really good mixing and enough time to dissolve so your frosting will be smooth and creamy like the candy.

1 cup (packed) dark brown sugar

3 tablespoons heavy whipping cream

2 cups (4 sticks) unsalted butter, at room temperature

½ teaspoon vanilla extract

½ teaspoon butterscotch extract

BUTTERSCOTCH FROSTING

∴ **MAKES ENOUGH FOR ONE 9-INCH 2-LAYER CAKE OR 1 DOZEN CUPCAKES**

1   In a small bowl, stir together the brown sugar and cream. Let sit until the sugar has dissolved, 15 to 20 minutes. Stir again.

2   In the bowl of a stand mixer fitted with the paddle attachment, beat the butter on high speed until very smooth, 1 minute. Add the sugar mixture and both extracts. Beat on high speed until smooth, 5 minutes. Refrigerate for 30 minutes before using. The frosting will keep in an airtight container in the refrigerator for 2 to 3 days.

This is my favorite frosting for Chocolate Cake (page 25). As a kid, there was something special about getting to lick the beaters and use my fingers to get all of the frosting out of the bowl. My grown children still fight over them. I'm not sure if it's because of how yummy this frosting truly is, or if it's the happy memories it brings up that make it my favorite frosting—probably a little of both. Either way, this white frosting will make any cake taste wonderful and look beautiful. Whip up a batch and see for yourself. You can even lick the beaters.

6 large egg whites, at room temperature

1 teaspoon baking powder

2 cups sugar

1 teaspoon white vinegar

WHITE FROSTING

∴ MAKES ENOUGH FOR THE MIDDLES AND EXTERIOR OF ONE 9-INCH 4-LAYER CAKE OR 2 DOZEN CUPCAKES

1   In the bowl of a stand mixer fitted with the whisk attachment, beat the egg whites on high speed until stiff, 4 to 5 minutes. Add the baking powder and beat on high speed just to combine.

2   Meanwhile, in a 2-quart heavy-bottomed saucepan set over medium heat, whisk together the sugar, vinegar, and 1 cup water. Cook until the mixture comes to a rapid boil and appears to be spinning a thread in the center of the pan, 6 to 8 minutes.

3   With the mixer on high speed, slowly pour the hot sugar mixture into the egg whites. Continue beating on high speed until the frosting is stiff enough to hold its shape, 8 to 10 minutes. The frosting will keep in an airtight container in the refrigerator for only 1 to 2 days before it starts to break down.

If you don't have time to make Aunt Daisy's Cooked Coconut Filling (page 141), this is a nice substitute. The coconut milk and frozen coconut make it very flavorful. This is the same recipe I use in my CoCo-Mo' Cake and the one I recommend to use along with the Yellow Cake (page 21) and the Orange Curd (page 146) for a taste reminiscent of ambrosia.

COCONUT FROSTING

·.·. **MAKES ENOUGH FOR ONE 9-INCH 4-LAYER CAKE OR 2 DOZEN CUPCAKES**

¼ cup coconut milk, plus more as needed

1 teaspoon vanilla extract

1 teaspoon coconut extract

2 cups (4 sticks) unsalted butter, at room temperature

6 ounces fresh-frozen shredded or grated coconut, thawed

6 cups confectioners' sugar

1 cup sweetened coconut flakes

1   In a small bowl, combine the coconut milk and both extracts.

2   In the bowl of a stand mixer fitted with the paddle attachment, beat the butter on high speed until smooth, about 2 minutes. Add the thawed coconut and blend well. With the mixer on the lowest speed setting, gradually add the confectioners' sugar, a cup at a time, alternately with the coconut milk mixture. When combined, beat on high speed for 1 minute. If the frosting is a little stiff, add more coconut milk, 1 teaspoon at a time, until it is fairly loose and easily spreadable. It is best to use this frosting right away. It hardens quickly when put into the refrigerator and requires bringing to room temperature and remixing in order to spread.

3   After spreading the frosting, press the sweetened coconut flakes onto the sides and over the top of the cake.

This is the ganache we use at Daisy Cakes between our cake layers and in some of our frostings, except that we make it in giant gallon-sized batches! It's a great recipe using either dark or white chocolate, and it's good as a drizzle over cupcakes and cookies, too.

2 cups heavy whipping cream

¼ cup light corn syrup

4 cups semisweet chocolate chips or white chocolate chips

CHOCOLATE GANACHE

⋱ **MAKES 5½ CUPS**

1   In a 2-quart heavy-bottomed saucepan set over medium-high heat, heat the cream until it foams up the sides of the saucepan, 8 to 10 minutes. Whisk in the corn syrup until completely blended. Remove the pan from the heat and add the chocolate chips.

2   Let sit until the chips melt, 5 minutes. Whisk until smooth. I chill the ganache in the fridge, uncovered, for 3 to 4 hours so that it thickens before using. The ganache will keep in an airtight container in the refrigerator for 7 to 10 days.

Variations

MOCHA GANACHE   Add 2 tablespoons espresso powder to the scalded cream along with the corn syrup.

MINT GANACHE   To a white chocolate ganache, add 1½ teaspoons of mint extract and 2 drops of green food coloring.

This adults-only glaze is the perfect drizzle for a pound cake, cupcakes, or ice cream. Be sure to spoon it on while the cake is still warm.

MOONSHINE GLAZE

⫶ MAKES ¾ CUP

1 cup confectioners' sugar, sifted

2 to 3 tablespoons moonshine, plain or apple pie-flavored (or bourbon)

2 teaspoons vanilla extract

¼ teaspoon ground cinnamon (optional)

In a small bowl, whisk together the confectioners' sugar, moonshine, vanilla, and cinnamon, if using, until smooth. The glaze will keep up to 1 month in the refrigerator.

This whipped cream is a perfect topping for cakes or cupcakes where you might want a lighter alternative to a cream cheese or buttercream frosting. I like it between the layers of cake when I don't want to frost the outside. I love it as big dollop on my favorite Apple-Walnut Pound Cake (page 32) and on just about any pie.

2 cups heavy whipping cream

½ cup confectioners' sugar

½ teaspoon vanilla extract

WHIPPED CREAM

·∵· MAKES 4 CUPS

1   In the chilled bowl of a stand mixer fitted with a chilled whisk attachment, beat the whipping cream, confectioners' sugar, and vanilla on high speed until stiff peaks form, 4 minutes.

2   Use immediately or store in an airtight container in the refrigerator for up to 3 days, and whisk lightly before using.

> **HINT**   As a rule of thumb, I generally use 2 tablespoons of confectioners' sugar for every 1 cup of whipping cream when making a whipped-cream topping or frosting.

Variation

FLAVORED WHIPPED CREAM   Any of your favorite extract flavors will work well in place of vanilla in the whipped cream, including your favorite liqueur. I suggest increasing the liqueur to 1 to 2 teaspoons.

Though not a sip of liquor ever passed her lips, Mama Bishop would have been just fine with this rum sauce as long as the rum was cooked out of it. You can make it either way, so take your pick. This sauce also keeps nicely in the fridge; warm it up and drizzle it over your favorite ice cream, especially the rum raisin (page 203).

½ cup (1 stick) unsalted butter

½ cup (packed) dark brown sugar

½ cup dark spiced rum

BUTTERED RUM SAUCE

∴ **MAKES 1¼ CUPS**

In a 1-quart saucepan set over medium-high heat, melt the butter. Add the brown sugar and cook, stirring constantly, until dissolved, 5 minutes. Remove the pan from the heat and whisk in the rum. If you want the alcohol to evaporate, cook over medium-high heat, stirring constantly, for 5 minutes, or to thicken, reduce the heat and cook for an additional 5 minutes. The sauce will keep in an airtight container in the refrigerator up to 2 weeks. It is best to reheat it before serving.

This strawberry sauce is perfect as a filling between yellow (page 21) or chocolate cake layers (page 25). It's also delicious over ice cream, and a jar of it makes a nice hostess gift, too. Other seasonal fruits—blackberries, blueberries, peaches, and pineapple—also work great in this recipe. But be sure to adjust the sugar, since each fruit has a different level of sweetness.

¼ cup cornstarch

1 cup cold water

2 cups sugar

4 cups hulled and sliced fresh strawberries

Pinch of salt

STRAWBERRY SAUCE

⋮ **MAKE 2 PINTS**

1   In a small bowl, dissolve the cornstarch in the cold water.

2   In a 1½-quart heavy-bottomed saucepan set over medium heat, combine the sugar, strawberries, and salt. Cook, stirring constantly, until hot, 10 minutes. Stir in the cornstarch mixture. Cover, reduce the heat to low, and cook, stirring occasionally, until thickened, 15 minutes. The sauce will keep in the refrigerator in an airtight container for 1 week, or freeze it to enjoy later.

If there's one thing my family loves most of all, it's a bowl of ice cream with chocolate sauce on it. We tend to use a small ramekin so we don't eat too much. It's funny how three or four small ramekins of ice cream just doesn't seem to add up to the same amount as a regular bowl.

1 cup sugar

¼ cup Dutch-processed cocoa powder

Pinch of salt

½ cup half-and-half or heavy whipping cream

¼ cup (½ stick) unsalted butter

½ teaspoon vanilla extract

CHOCOLATE SAUCE

∴ **MAKES 1 PINT**

1 In a 1-quart heavy-bottomed saucepan set over medium heat, add the sugar, cocoa, salt, half-and-half, and butter. Cook, whisking constantly, until the sugar is dissolved, the butter is melted, and the mixture starts to thicken, 8 to 10 minutes.

2 Remove the pan from the heat. Stir in the vanilla. Serve this sauce warm or cold. It will keep in an airtight container in the refrigerator for 1 week. Warm the sauce before serving.

> **HINT** I heat only the amount I want to use in a ramekin for 15 to 20 seconds in the microwave.

Variation

MOCHA SAUCE Add 2 teaspoons espresso powder after removing the sauce from the heat. Stir to dissolve.

SPIKED CHOCOLATE SAUCE Reduce the amount of half-and-half by 2 tablespoons. After removing the pan from the heat, stir in 2 table-spoons dark rum, bourbon, or moonshine.

Although I love a hot fudge sundae with lots of whipped cream and nuts, the perfect way to enjoy this fudge sauce is on a sliver of leftover pound cake with a big scoop of ice cream. Don't forget the cherry on top!

1 12-ounce can sweetened condensed milk

¾ cup mini semisweet chocolate chips

1 tablespoon heavy cream

1 tablespoon unsalted butter

1 teaspoon vanilla extract

FUDGE SAUCE

·∴· **MAKES 1¾ CUPS**

1 In a 1½-quart heavy-bottomed saucepan set over medium heat, combine the condensed milk, chocolate chips, and heavy cream, stirring constantly until the chocolate chips are melted and the mixture is smooth, 5 minutes. Remove from the heat. Whisk in the butter and vanilla.

2 Serve warm or store in the refrigerator in an airtight container for up to 1 week. Reheat before serving.

Variations

MOCHA FUDGE SAUCE For a mocha sauce, stir 1 teaspoon espresso powder into the condensed milk mixture while heating.

ORANGE FUDGE SAUCE After removing from the heat, add ¼ teaspoon orange extract along with 2 teaspoons grated orange zest for a more decadent fudge sauce.

I love everything about pumpkin. This filling is so light and fluffy, but at the same time, it has a rich flavor from the spices. It's very versatile and easy to make. Try it as the filling for the Pumpkin Whoopee Pies (page 82) or in the Pumpkin Roll (page 64), Vanilla Cake Roll (page 61), or even the Pecan Roll (page 63). I also love to scatter pieces of toffee over the filling!

2 cups heavy whipping cream, cold

1 cup sugar

1 8-ounce package cream cheese, cold

1 15-ounce can 100% pure pumpkin puree, cold

½ teaspoon pumpkin pie spice, or more to taste

WHIPPED PUMPKIN FILLING

·∴· MAKES 4 CUPS

In the chilled bowl of a stand mixer fitted with a chilled whisk attachment, beat the whipping cream and sugar on high speed until peaks form, about 3 minutes. Beat in the cream cheese, pumpkin, and pumpkin pie spice until smooth, about 1 minute. Cover and refrigerate until ready to use.

I remember my Aunt Daisy cracking open and grating fresh coconuts for this recipe. She would then stand over the stove, stirring this filling for what seemed like the entire day! You don't have to crack your own coconuts and grate them—unless you just want to—but you will need to make sure you have about 2 hours to devote to this recipe. It's worth it and out of this world! Use it to fill yellow (page 21) or chocolate (page 25) cake layers, which are then frosted with Coconut Frosting (page 130), Vanilla Buttercream Frosting (page 126), or Chocolate Frosting (page 118), and coat the outside with 2 cups sweetened coconut flakes so that it's nice and fluffy.

1 heaping tablespoon cornstarch

½ cup whole milk

1 cup (2 sticks) unsalted butter

2 12-ounce cans evaporated milk

2½ cups sugar

1 tablespoon vanilla extract

Pinch of salt

2 6-ounce packs fresh-frozen shredded or grated coconut, thawed

aunt daisy's
COOKED COCONUT FILLING

MAKES ENOUGH FILLING FOR ONE 9-INCH 3-LAYER CAKE

1 In a small bowl, dissolve the cornstarch in the cold milk.

2 In a cast-iron skillet set over medium heat, melt the butter. Add the evaporated milk and heat slightly. Add the sugar and cook, stirring constantly, until hot, 5 minutes. Gradually add the cornstarch mixture, stirring well. Reduce the heat to low, pull up a stool, and cook, stirring constantly, until the filling is thickened and coats the back of a spoon, 1 hour and 20 minutes.

3 Prepare a shallow pan of ice water large enough to hold the skillet.

4 Remove the skillet from the heat and stir in the vanilla and salt. Place the skillet in the ice water and let it sit, stirring occasionally, until cool, 45 minutes.

5 Stir the thawed coconut into the cooled filling. The filling will keep in an airtight container in the refrigerator for up to 1 week.

One of my biggest thrills was being invited to cook on the Today *show. Even though I knew Al Roker's favorite cake is red velvet, I wanted to bring a taste of South Carolina along with me. I chose peaches and made them into this recipe. In case you're wondering, I took along a red velvet cake for Al, too.*

PEACHES FOSTER

∴ **SERVES 12 TO 16**

½ cup (1 stick) unsalted butter

1 cup (packed) light brown sugar

6 to 8 large, ripe peaches, peeled and sliced

½ cup brandy

Ground cinnamon (optional)

1 cup coarsely chopped pecans, toasted (see Hint, page 42)

¼ cup (½ stick) unsalted butter, melted

½ teaspoon kosher salt

1   In a large skillet set over medium heat, melt the ½ cup butter and stir in the brown sugar until dissolved. Add the peaches and cook until just heated through. Remove from the heat.

2   Dim the lights. Add the brandy to the skillet and ignite it. A sprinkle of cinnamon, if using, over the flaming skillet will add some sparkle to the flame.

3   In a small bowl, toss the toasted pecans with the ¼ cup melted butter and salt. (The nuts will keep in the refrigerator for a month in an airtight container.)

4   Serve the peaches over your favorite ice cream with the toasted pecans sprinkled on top. I love serving these warm peaches over the Buttermilk Ice Cream (page 212).

This is the lemon curd I use between the layers of my Love Dat Lemon cake. I make it in small batches in my grandmother's yellow enamel pot, which cooks it perfectly every time. Make sure you have time to give this recipe your full attention because it cannot be left unattended and will scorch easily without constant stirring. You'll also want to be sure to zest your lemons before juicing them. It's much easier to juice a zested lemon than to zest a juiced one.

4 large eggs

8 large egg yolks

1½ cups sugar

1 cup fresh lemon juice (about 8 large lemons)

1 to 2 tablespoons grated lemon zest

LEMON CURD

·ᛉ· MAKES 2 CUPS

1   Keep an 8 × 8 × 2-inch glass baking dish nearby, along with a rubber spatula and plastic wrap.

2   In a 2-quart heavy-bottomed saucepan, whisk the eggs and yolks until combined. Whisk in the sugar. Whisk in the lemon juice until smooth. Set the pan over medium heat and cook, whisking constantly, until the curd is thick and the foam on the surface has been incorporated into the curd, 12 to 15 minutes (reduce the heat if the custard begins to scorch). Remove the pan from the heat. Stir in the zest, making sure it's evenly distributed and doesn't clump up.

3   Pour the curd into the baking dish, using the rubber spatula to scrape all the curd out of the saucepan. Cover the curd with the plastic wrap, making sure that the plastic touches the entire surface to prevent a thick, rubbery film from forming. Refrigerate until cool, at least 3 to 4 hours or overnight. The curd will keep in the refrigerator for a week. It also freezes beautifully.

> **HINT**   When making a curd or any type of cooked egg custard or filling, be sure to remove the chalaza—the white band-like membrane on each end of the yolk—to keep the custard smooth and creamy. If left in the egg, the chalaza will cook and become a chewy little bit that prevents the custard from having a silky texture. Leaving the chalaza in will not affect the taste, only the texture.

Variation

LIME CURD   Substitute 1 tablespoon grated lime zest and 1 of fresh lime juice in place of the lemon zest and juice.

If I'm not having chocolate, my choice for dessert will always be something made with citrus. It's so light and refreshing. This curd is made differently from the lemon and lime curds, because of the sugar in the orange juice. By adding the lemon juice and gelatin, the curd will thicken and set up nicely. The added lemon juice also brightens the curd and gives it a nice bit of tartness. Don't forget to zest your oranges before juicing them. If you do forget, it's a lesson you'll need to learn only one time.

¼ cup fresh lemon juice (2 to 3 lemons)

1 tablespoon unflavored gelatin

4 large eggs

8 large egg yolks

1½ cups sugar

1 cup fresh orange juice

¼ cup grated orange zest

ORANGE CURD

∴ **MAKES 2 CUPS**

1   Keep an 8 × 8 × 2-inch glass baking dish nearby, along with a rubber spatula and plastic wrap.

2   Put the lemon juice in a small bowl and sprinkle the gelatin over it. Let sit for 15 minutes, while the curd is cooking.

3   In a 2-quart heavy-bottomed saucepan, whisk together the eggs and yolks. Whisk in the sugar. Whisk in the orange juice until smooth. Set the pan over medium heat and cook, whisking constantly, until thick and the foam on the surface has been incorporated into the curd, 12 to 15 minutes (reduce the heat if the custard begins to scorch). Remove the pan from the heat. Whisk in the gelatin mixture until smooth. Stir in the zest, making sure it's evenly distributed and doesn't clump up.

4   Pour the curd into the baking dish, using the rubber spatula to scrape all of the curd out of the saucepan. Cover the curd with the plastic wrap, making sure that the plastic touches the entire surface to prevent a thick, rubbery film from forming. Refrigerate until cool, at least 3 to 4 hours or overnight.

HINT   For a combination that reminds me of a delicious bowl of ambrosia, use the orange curd to fill yellow cake layers (page 21) and frost the cake with the Coconut Frosting (page 130). Garnish with mandarin orange segments for a nice touch.

PIES
and
fritters

I can still hear my grandmothers and great-aunt giving me all sorts of advice, from words of wisdom to old wives' tales concerning cooking and life. Two of those phrases that apply to this chapter are (1) don't overwork your dough, and (2) don't overmix your batter. Overworking the dough will make it tough, and overmixing the batter will make the fritters too dense and heavy. These are words to bake by from three of the best cooks I've ever known!

Just like cookies, pies and fritters can feed the masses if you need them to. My pie recipes are easily doubled as well, and should you need to serve a "gracious plenty," simply triple the recipe and make it into a gracious plenty pie that can serve 24 to 30 people, depending on how you cut it.

One of my earliest kitchen memories is sitting on my knees on my little yellow stool while Mama Bishop and Aunt Daisy taught me how to roll out dough. They rolled dough with a smooth rhythm that seemed to come to them as easily as breathing. The patience they showed throughout all the messes I made seemed the same. These days, I find rolling dough so soothing that it's almost therapeutic.

BASIC PIECRUST

·∴· MAKES ONE 9-INCH, 10-INCH, OR DEEP-DISH PIECRUST

1 cup unbleached all-purpose flour, plus more for rolling

¼ teaspoon salt

¼ cup (½ stick) unsalted butter, cut into cubes, cold

2 tablespoons vegetable shortening, cold

1 teaspoon white vinegar

3 to 4 tablespoons ice water

Nonstick cooking spray

1 Sift the flour and salt into the bowl of a food processor fitted with the blade attachment. Add the butter and shortening, and pulse until the mixture has a cornmeal-like consistency, eight to ten pulses. With the food processor running, gradually add the vinegar and the ice water, 1 tablespoon at a time, until the dough comes together in a ball. Transfer the dough to a sheet of plastic wrap, flatten it into a disk, cover, and refrigerate for 30 minutes.

2 To bake the crust, preheat the oven to 425°F.

3 On a lightly floured surface, roll the dough out into a 12-inch circle. Carefully place the dough into a 9-inch pie plate, trim the overhang, and prick the bottom and sides with a fork. Cover the dough completely with foil that's sprayed lightly with nonstick cooking spray and fill with pie weights or dried beans.

4 Bake for 8 to 10 minutes. Remove the foil and pie weights, and bake until the crust is golden brown, 4 to 5 more minutes.

HINT The secret to perfect piecrust is *to not overwork the dough* or it will be tough! Pulse it in the food processor just until it comes together in a ball.

My granddaddy Papa Bishop raised cows and hogs. There were always hams hanging in the smokehouse, lard that was rendered for cooking, and milk being churned for butter. Mama Bishop and Aunt Daisy used only the churned butter and lard from my granddaddy's cows and hogs for all of their baking and cooking. Lard absolutely makes the flakiest and best piecrust you will ever put in your mouth. However, you can substitute vegetable shortening, and it'll taste just fine. Of course, my grandmothers and great-aunt didn't have a food processor to use for their pie dough—they made it using their hands in a dough bowl. Thank goodness for modern-day inventions!

1½ cups unbleached all-purpose flour, plus more for rolling

2 tablespoons sugar

½ teaspoon salt

¼ cup (½ stick) unsalted butter, cut into cubes, cold

2 tablespoons lard, cold

6 to 8 tablespoons ice water

SOUTHERN-STYLE PIECRUST

∴ MAKES ONE 9-INCH PIECRUST

1   Combine the flour, sugar, and salt in the bowl of a food processor fitted with the blade attachment. Pulse once or twice. Add the cold butter and lard. Pulse until the mixture has a cornmeal-like consistency, eight to ten pulses. Add 2 tablespoons of the ice water and pulse a few times. With the food processor running, add the remaining ice water, a tablespoon at a time, just until the dough comes together into a ball. Transfer the dough to a piece of waxed paper or plastic wrap. Knead it with the heel of your hand five or six times. Form the dough into a disk, wrap it up, and refrigerate for 30 minutes.

2   To bake the crust, preheat the oven to 425°F.

3   On a lightly floured surface, roll the dough out into a 12-inch circle. Carefully place the dough into a 9-inch pie plate, trim the overhang, and prick the bottom and sides with a fork. Cover the dough completely with foil and fill with pie weights or dried beans.

4   Bake for 10 to 12 minutes. Carefully remove the foil and pie weights, and bake until the crust is golden brown, 4 to 5 more minutes.

When you just can't get enough chocolate in your pie, add some chocolate to your dough, too! This is the perfect crust for the Chocolate Chess Pie (page 159).

CHOCOLATE PIECRUST

¼ cup semisweet mini chocolate chips

1½ cups unbleached all-purpose flour

2 teaspoons sugar

¼ teaspoon salt

½ cup (1 stick) unsalted butter, cut into cubes, cold

∴ **MAKES ONE 9-INCH, 10-INCH, OR DEEP-DISH PIECRUST**

1   In a microwave-safe glass measuring cup, microwave the chocolate chips in 3 tablespoons water on high until melted, 1 to 2 minutes. Stir until smooth. Let cool slightly.

2   Sift together the flour, sugar, and salt in the bowl of a stand mixer fitted with the paddle attachment. Add the butter and beat on low speed until the flour is the consistency of cornmeal. Drizzle in the cooled melted chocolate. Beat on low speed until combined. Increase the speed to medium-high and beat for 30 seconds.

3   Transfer the dough to a sheet of waxed paper and top with a second sheet. Work the dough into a ball, flatten it into a disk, and refrigerate for 1 to 2 hours.

4   Roll the dough out between the wax paper sheets into a 10- or 11-inch circle depending on the size of the pie pan. Carefully press the dough into a 9- or 10-inch pie pan. Prick the bottom and sides of the dough with a fork and refrigerate for 30 minutes.

5   Preheat the oven to 375°F.

6   Bake until the crust is set, 15 to 18 minutes. Let cool completely before filling.

This cookie crust is ideal for gracious plenty pies or homemade ice cream sandwiches. Its simple flavor allows you to really go all out on your choice of filling or ice cream.

COOKIE CRUST

∴ **MAKES ONE 12 × 18-INCH CRUST OR TWO 9-INCH PIECRUSTS**

1   Preheat the oven to 325°F. Coat a 12 × 18 × 1-inch half-sheet pan or two 9-inch pie plates with Pan Grease (page 16) or butter or shortening with a light dusting of flour.

2   In a medium bowl, sift together the flour, baking soda, cream of tartar, and salt.

3   In the bowl of a stand mixer fitted with the paddle attachment, beat together the butter and both sugars on high speed until smooth, 2 minutes. Beat in the egg and vanilla. Scrape down the sides and around the bottom of the bowl. Continue beating on high speed for 1 more minute. Add the flour mixture and beat on low speed just until combined. Scrape down the bowl. Beat on high speed for 30 seconds. Using lightly floured hands, press the dough evenly into the prepared pan, being sure to get into the corners and up the sides of the half-sheet pan.

4   Bake until golden brown, 15 to 18 minutes. Let cool just to room temperature if you plan on cutting the crust to use for ice cream sandwiches; cut it with a cookie cutter, place uncovered on a clean half-sheet pan, and freeze until ready to use with the ice cream. If you plan on topping the crust with a filling, let it cool completely.

Pan Grease (page 16) or extra butter or shortening and flour for preparing the pan or pie plates

2½ cups unbleached all-purpose flour, plus more for your hands

2 teaspoons baking soda

2 teaspoons cream of tartar

½ teaspoon salt

1 cup (2 sticks) unsalted butter, at room temperature

1 cup confectioners' sugar

¼ cup granulated sugar

1 large egg

1 teaspoon vanilla extract

Variations

CHOCOLATE CHIP OR PECAN COOKIE CRUST   Press 2 cups of semisweet chocolate chips or toasted chopped pecans into the crust before baking.

CHOCOLATE COOKIE CRUST   For a chocolate crust, sift ¾ cup Dutch-processed cocoa powder in with the flour, increase the number of large eggs to 2, and add ½ teaspoon chocolate extract. Bake for 20 to 22 minutes.

ICE CREAM PIE   For a "gracious plenty" ice cream pie, spread your choice of ice cream over the crust as you would a pie filling.

If you're making a pie with a fruit filling that might not be as sweet as a custard filling, this pie dough is the one to use. It has a nice flavor and a good texture that won't become overly soggy from the juices produced by the cooked fruit. A light dusting of flour over the crust before adding the fruit filling helps, too.

SWEET PIECRUST

·∴· **MAKES ONE 9-INCH, 10-INCH, OR DEEP-DISH PIECRUST**

1½ cups unbleached all-purpose flour, plus more for rolling

3 tablespoons sugar

½ teaspoon salt

½ cup (1 stick) unsalted butter, cut into cubes, cold

1 large egg yolk

1½ teaspoons white vinegar

1   Sift the flour, sugar, and salt into a large bowl and then transfer it to a food processor fitted with the blade attachment. Add the butter and pulse until the mixture has a cornmeal-like consistency, eight to ten pulses. With the food processor running, add the egg yolk and vinegar, and continue processing just until the dough forms a ball. Transfer the dough to a sheet of waxed paper and top with a second sheet. Flatten the dough into a disk and refrigerate for 30 minutes.

2   To bake the crust, preheat the oven to 425°F.

3   Remove the waxed paper from the dough. On a lightly floured surface, roll the dough out into a 12-inch circle. Carefully place the dough into a 9-inch pie plate, trim the overhang, and prick the bottom and sides with a fork. Cover the dough completely with foil and fill with pie weights or dried beans.

4   Bake for 8 to 10 minutes. Remove the foil and pie weights, and bake until the crust is golden brown, 4 to 5 more minutes.

I love to pair fresh berries with almonds in my baked goods. Sometimes I add a touch of almond extract and toasted almonds, but other times I'll use this crust. There's just something about almond flavor that gives the fruit a warm and comforting balance. I particularly love this crust with my Strawberry-Rhubarb-Basil Pie (page 169).

½ cup slivered almonds, toasted (see Hint, page 42)

1 cup unbleached all-purpose flour, plus more for rolling the dough

½ cup (packed) light brown sugar

¾ cup (1½ sticks) unsalted butter, at room temperature

ALMOND PIECRUST

∴ MAKES ONE 8 × 8-INCH PIECRUST OR ONE 9-INCH PIE CRUST

1   In the bowl of the food processor fitted with the blade attachment, finely grind the almonds. Add the flour and brown sugar, and pulse just to combine, five or six times. With the processor running, add the butter and continue to blend until the dough comes together in a ball.

2   Transfer the dough to a sheet of waxed paper and top with a second sheet. Press the dough into a disk and refrigerate for 30 minutes.

3   On a lightly floured surface, roll the dough to the desired size. You can use it as a bottom crust or top crust—or both if you double the recipe! It is not necessary to bake this piecrust before adding the filling.

Southern folklore has a few ideas about where the name "chess pie" came from. I have always heard two explanations. One is that chess pie is made with ingredients a cook would always have on hand, either in the icebox or the pie chest, or "chess" as many Southerners pronounce it. Another explanation is that, because of the amount of sugar used, the pie could be kept in the pie chest (chess) and not in the icebox after baking. One thing everyone can agree on is that sometimes it's the simple things that taste the best.

CHESS PIE

∴ MAKES ONE 9-INCH PIE

1   Preheat the oven to 375°F.

2   In the bowl of a stand mixer fitted with the whisk attachment, beat the sugar and butter on high speed until smooth and creamy, 5 minutes. Add the eggs and beat on high speed for 1 minute. Scrape down the sides and around the bottom of the bowl. Add the cornmeal, milk, vinegar, vanilla, and salt. Beat on high speed for 1 more minute. Pour the mixture into the unbaked piecrust.

3   Bake for 10 minutes. Without opening the oven door, reduce the heat to 325°F and continue baking until the custard is set, 35 to 40 more minutes. Let cool completely before serving.

1½ cups sugar

½ cup (1 stick) unsalted butter, at room temperature

4 large eggs

2 tablespoons cornmeal

2 tablespoons whole milk

1 tablespoon white vinegar

1 teaspoon vanilla extract

Pinch of salt

1 chilled and unbaked Basic Piecrust (page 150) or Southern-Style Piecrust (page 152), fitted into a 9-inch pie plate

Just as sure as the sun rises in the morning, I always knew while growing up that I could count on coming home from church on any given Sunday to find a table full of the best food I would ever put in my mouth. While Aunt Daisy was putting the ice into the tea glasses and Mama Bishop was finishing up the gravy, I couldn't help but sneak a peek into the pie chest to see what was for dessert. I always hoped that it would be this one!

CHOCOLATE CHESS PIE

∴ MAKES ONE 9-INCH PIE

1½ cups sugar

¼ cup Dutch-processed cocoa powder

3 large eggs

¾ cup evaporated milk

1 teaspoon vanilla extract

¼ cup (½ stick) unsalted butter, melted

1 chilled and unbaked Sweet Piecrust (page 150) or Chocolate Piecrust (page 153), fitted into a 9-inch pie plate

1   Preheat the oven to 350°F.

2   In the bowl of a stand mixer fitted with the whisk attachment, beat the sugar and the cocoa on low speed to blend, 15 seconds. Add the eggs, evaporated milk, vanilla, and melted butter, and beat on low speed just to combine. Scrape down the sides and around the bottom of the bowl. Beat on high speed for 1 minute. Pour into the unbaked piecrust.

3   Bake until firm, 45 to 50 minutes. Let cool completely before serving.

Mama Bishop and Aunt Daisy both had their own chicken pens. They had a friendly little competition to see whose hens would lay the most eggs every day—and who made the best pies, too. We had a great time baking with those country eggs. There is nothing like using them to bake with and no denying the difference fresh eggs make in this pie; the yolks of fresh eggs give it a beautiful yellow color that is matched perfectly by the brightness of the fresh lemon juice. The custard is sweet, rich, and creamy with a tangy zip—all at the same time.

LEMON CHESS PIE

·⋮· MAKES ONE 9-INCH PIE

½ cup (1 stick) unsalted butter, at room temperature

1½ cups sugar

4 large eggs

2 tablespoons cornmeal

¼ cup fresh lemon juice

1 teaspoon vanilla extract

Pinch of salt

2 teaspoons grated lemon zest

1 chilled and unbaked Sweet Piecrust (page 156) or Southern-Style Piecrust (page 152), fitted into a 9-inch pie plate

1   Preheat the oven to 400°F.

2   In the bowl of a stand mixer fitted with the whisk attachment, beat the butter and the sugar on high speed until smooth and creamy, 3 minutes. Add the eggs and beat just to combine. Scrape down the sides and around the bottom of the bowl. Beat on high speed for 2 minutes. Add the cornmeal, lemon juice, vanilla, and salt, and beat on high speed for 1 minute. Using a rubber spatula, fold in the lemon zest. Pour the custard into the unbaked piecrust.

3   Bake for 10 minutes. Without opening the oven door, reduce the temperature to 325°F and bake until the custard is set and firm, 30 to 35 more minutes. Let cool completely before serving.

As a Southern gal with plenty of pecans in the freezer and the basics in the fridge, I can make just about any dessert at a moment's notice. If you don't have any buttermilk on hand, don't fret. Just add 1 tablespoon of white vinegar to your measuring cup, fill it to the 1 cup line with whole milk, and you're set. The streusel-like topping on this pie gives it a perfect crunch to go along with the creamy custard filling and rich flavor. A little dollop of whipped cream or a scoop of vanilla ice cream is nice, too.

PECAN CRUMBLE CHESS PIE

∴ MAKES ONE 9-INCH PIE

1 **Prepare the topping:** In a medium bowl, combine the flour and brown sugar. Cut in the butter until the mixture is the consistency of cornmeal. Work in the pecans so they get some of the sugar coating on them. Set aside.

2 Preheat the oven to 425°F.

3 **Make the filling:** In the bowl of a stand mixer fitted with the whisk attachment, beat the butter and sugar on high speed until smooth and creamy, 3 minutes. Add the flour and beat just to combine. Add the eggs and beat on high speed for 1 minute. Scrape down the sides and around the bottom of the bowl. Beat on high speed for 1 more minute. Add the buttermilk and the vanilla, and beat on high speed for 1 minute. Pour the filling into the unbaked piecrust.

4 Bake for 10 minutes. Without opening the oven door, reduce the heat to 350°F and bake for 20 more minutes. Remove the pie from the oven and sprinkle the pecan topping evenly over the top. Return the pie to the oven and bake until the filling is set, 15 to 20 minutes. Serve warm or at room temperature.

PECAN TOPPING

¼ cup unbleached all-purpose flour

¼ cup (packed) dark brown sugar

¼ cup (½ stick) unsalted butter, at room temperature

1 cup coarsely chopped pecans

FILLING

½ cup (1 stick) unsalted butter, at room temperature

1½ cups sugar

¼ cup unbleached all-purpose flour

4 large eggs

1 cup buttermilk, at room temperature

1 teaspoon vanilla extract

1 chilled and unbaked Basic Piecrust (page 150) or Southern-Style Piecrust (page 152), fitted into a 9-inch pie plate

You might be surprised to find out that vinegar in pie can be a good thing. It actually balances out the sweetness of the sugar and makes the custard extra creamy. I prefer apple cider vinegar, since it has more flavor and punch than regular white vinegar. Make this pie and see for yourself that when it comes to a creamy egg custard dessert, one with vinegar in it really delivers.

VINEGAR CHESS PIE

· ⋮ · MAKES ONE 9-INCH PIE

1 Preheat the oven to 300°F.

2 In the bowl of a stand mixer fitted with the whisk attachment, beat the sugar and the butter on low speed until smooth and creamy, 3 minutes. Add the eggs and beat on high speed for 1 minute. Scrape down the sides and around the bottom of the bowl. Add the flour, vinegar, and vanilla. Beat on high speed for 2 minutes. Pour into the unbaked piecrust.

3 Bake until the custard is set and firm, 1 hour. Cool completely before serving.

1½ cups sugar

½ cup (1 stick) unsalted butter, melted

3 large eggs

2 tablespoons unbleached all-purpose flour

2 tablespoons apple cider vinegar

1 tablespoon vanilla extract

1 chilled and unbaked Basic Piecrust (page 150), fitted into a 9-inch pie plate

One of my cooking students was nice enough to share this recipe with me. I remember the first time I tried it; I was delighted by how nicely the rum and chocolate flavors worked together. It's light and delicious, and perfect for your book club or garden club gathering. You can make it ahead of time, too.

CHOCOLATE RUM PIE

·∴· MAKES TWO 9-INCH DEEP-DISH PIES
   OR ONE 12 × 18 × 1-INCH PIE

¼ cup cold water

2 teaspoons unflavored gelatin

2 large eggs, separated

¾ cup whole milk

¼ cup plus 2 teaspoons dark rum

¾ cup granulated sugar

Pinch of salt

¾ cup semisweet chocolate chips

2 cups heavy whipping cream

¼ cup confectioners' sugar

2 baked 9-inch deep-dish Basic Piecrusts (page 150) or Chocolate Piecrusts (page 153)

1   Pour the cold water into a small bowl and sprinkle the gelatin over it. Let sit for 5 minutes.

2   In a metal bowl set over a pan of simmering water or in a double boiler, whisk together the egg yolks, milk, and the ¼ cup rum. Add the dissolved gelatin, ¼ cup of the sugar, and the salt. Cook, whisking constantly, until slightly thickened, 10 to 12 minutes. Make sure the bottom of the bowl doesn't touch the water. Remove the bowl from the heat and add the chocolate chips. Let sit until the chips melt, 3 minutes. Whisk until blended. Refrigerate, uncovered, until cold and thickened slightly, 2 to 3 hours.

3   In the bowl of a stand mixer fitted with the whisk attachment, beat the egg whites on high speed until they form peaks, 3 minutes. With the mixer running on high speed, gradually add the remaining ½ cup sugar and continue beating until very stiff, 2 more minutes. Fold into the chilled chocolate mixture. Pour into the cooled crusts, equally divided. Wash, thoroughly dry, and then chill the bowl and whisk attachment in the freezer until they are very cold.

4   In the chilled bowl with the chilled whisk, beat the whipping cream, ¼ cup confectioners' sugar, and the remaining 2 teaspoons rum on high speed until thick peaks form, 5 minutes. Evenly divide the whipping cream between the pies and swirl it with a spoon to make pretty peaks. The whipped cream does not have to cover the entire pie. Refrigerate before serving, at least 3 to 4 hours or overnight.

If there's one thing I can pretty much guarantee, it's that nearly every Southern cook has two things: a chest freezer and a 5-pound bag (at least) of pecans in it. Now, we might not all agree on the correct pronunciation of these delicious meaty nuts, but there's no doubt we can all agree on how nice it is to have a bag or two in the freezer for when you need them. There are lots of pecan pie recipes in the world, too, but this is my favorite.

PECAN PIE

∴ MAKES ONE 9-INCH PIE

1 cup dark corn syrup

¾ cup sugar

½ cup (1 stick) unsalted butter, melted

½ teaspoon salt

4 large eggs

1 chilled and unbaked Basic Piecrust (page 150) or Chocolate Piecrust (page 153), fitted into a 9-inch pie plate

1½ cups pecan halves

1 Preheat the oven to 350°F.

2 In the bowl of a stand mixer fitted with the whisk attachment, beat the corn syrup, sugar, melted butter, and salt on high speed for 1 minute. Add the eggs and beat on high speed for 2 more minutes. Pour the mixture into the unbaked piecrust. Arrange the pecan halves over the top of the filling in a spiral design.

3 Bake until the pie filling is set and firm, 50 to 60 minutes. It will continue to set as it cools. Serve warm or at room temperature.

Variation

I like to press ½ cup of pecan pieces or chocolate chips into the bottom of the unbaked crust before adding the filling.

Every November the Junior League of Spartanburg holds its "Santa's Shoppe" and vendors come from all over the country to sell their specialty gifts to the holiday shoppers. As a Junior League member, I was always on the food committee. Every year we baked and sold what seemed like a thousand of these pies for people to take home and enjoy for Thanksgiving. Needless to say, we always ran out and left folks wanting more.

CHOCOLATE CHIP PECAN PIE

∴ MAKES ONE 9-INCH DEEP-DISH PIE

1 Preheat the oven to 350°F.

2 In the bowl of a stand mixer fitted with the whisk attachment, beat the sugar and butter on high speed until light and fluffy, 3 minutes. Add the eggs, the 2 tablespoons cream, and vanilla, and beat on high speed for 1 minute. Scrape down the sides and around the bottom of the bowl. Add the flour and salt. Beat on low speed just to combine. Increase the speed to high and beat for 1 minute.

3 Scatter the chocolate chips and pecans over the bottom of the baked piecrust. Spread the batter evenly over the chocolate chips and pecans. Wash, thoroughly dry, then chill the bowl and whisk attachment in the freezer until they are very cold.

4 Bake until the pie is golden brown and firm, 50 to 55 minutes. If the edges of the crust start to brown too quickly, cover the entire pie with a piece of aluminum foil until the pie is completely baked through. Cool completely. The pie will keep in the refrigerator up to 1 week. It also freezes nicely.

5 In the chilled bowl with the whisk attachment, beat the remaining 2 cups cream and the confectioners' sugar on high speed until stiff peaks form, 4 minutes. Serve on top of the pie.

2 cups granulated sugar

1 cup (2 sticks) unsalted butter, at room temperature

4 large eggs

2 cups plus 2 tablespoons heavy whipping cream

2 teaspoons vanilla extract

1 cup unbleached all-purpose flour, sifted

½ teaspoon salt

1½ cups semisweet chocolate chips

1½ cups chopped pecans, toasted (see Hint, page 42)

1 baked 9-inch deep dish Basic Piecrust (page 150)

¼ cup confectioners' sugar

I have a friend who makes an incredible strawberry-basil jelly. It's her jelly that gave me the idea for a modern-day twist to an old-fashioned diner classic. The basil and a splash of balsamic vinegar add a very unique and sophisticated element to this pie and make for a pleasant and tasty surprise. Since rhubarb is so tart, you'll want to sprinkle it with sugar and set it aside while getting the other ingredients together. Make sure your strawberries are nice and sweet, too.

STRAWBERRY-RHUBARB-BASIL PIE

∴ MAKES ONE 8 × 8-INCH PIE

1 Preheat the oven to 400°F. Lightly butter an 8 × 8 × 2-inch glass baking dish.

2 In a medium bowl, toss the rhubarb pieces with ½ cup of the sugar. Let stand for 30 minutes.

3 In a small bowl, whisk together the remaining 1 cup sugar, the cornstarch, and salt.

4 In a large bowl, toss together the strawberries, basil leaves, balsamic vinegar, and vanilla. Add the sugar mixture and stir well. Add the rhubarb. Pour the fruit mixture into the prepared baking dish. Dot with the butter and cover with the almond pie dough. Crimp the edges of the dough to seal it around the sides of the baking dish. Cut three or four slits in the dough to allow the steam to vent.

5 Bake until the crust is golden brown, 45 to 50 minutes. Serve warm or at room temperature.

2 tablespoons (¼ stick) unsalted butter, plus more for greasing the dish

3 cups ½-inch pieces of rhubarb

1½ cups sugar

¼ cup cornstarch

½ teaspoon salt

3 cups sliced fresh strawberries

½ cup torn fresh basil leaves

2 tablespoons balsamic vinegar

½ teaspoon vanilla extract

1 disk of unbaked Almond Piecrust (page 157) or Sweet Piecrust (page 156), cold or at room temperature and rolled to an 8-inch square on a lightly floured surface

If you've never been to hog heaven, it's because you haven't had a slice of this pie! It's cold, light, refreshing, and not too sweet—a perfect hot weather treat that will make you want to squeal with every bite!

BANANA SPLIT PIE

·∴· **MAKES ONE 9-INCH DEEP-DISH PIE**

1 Preheat the oven to 425°F. Line a 12 × 18 × 1-inch half-sheet pan with foil and spray with nonstick cooking spray. Spread the diced pineapple and halved bananas somewhat separated on the prepared pan.

2 In a 2-quart saucepan set over medium heat, melt the butter with the brown sugar, stirring until smooth. Drizzle the mixture over the pineapple and banana pieces. Roast until caramelized, 15 to 18 minutes. Let cool.

3 While the fruit cools, set the same saucepan over medium heat, and add the granulated sugar and flour. Whisk to blend. Add ¼ cup water and whisk until smooth. Add the roasted pineapple and cook, stirring occasionally, until thickened, 10 to 12 minutes. Let cool completely.

4 Line the baked piecrust with the roasted bananas. Pour the cooled pineapple mixture over the bananas.

5 In the chilled bowl of a stand mixer fitted with a chilled whisk, beat the cream, confectioners' sugar, and vanilla on high speed until stiff peaks form, 3 to 4 minutes. Spread over the bananas and pineapple. Just before serving, top with the moonshine-soaked cherries and wet walnuts, if using. Serve chilled.

Nonstick cooking spray

3 cups diced fresh pineapple

3 ripe yet firm bananas, halved lengthwise

¼ cup (½ stick) unsalted butter

½ cup (packed) dark brown sugar

½ cup granulated sugar

2 tablespoons unbleached all-purpose flour

1 baked 9-inch deep-dish Chocolate Piecrust (page 153) or Sweet Piecrust (page 156), at room temperature

2 cups heavy whipping cream

¼ cup confectioners' sugar

¼ teaspoon vanilla extract

Moonshine-Soaked Cherries (recipe follows, optional)

Wet Walnuts (recipe follows, optional)

recipe continues

For as long as I can remember, a man with one ear always came to visit Daddy for his birthday in May and again at Christmas. He drove an old jalopy without a tag and would only go in the house if no one else was in there except Daddy. He would leave a mason jar on the counter and not come back again for six months. I don't know whatever happened to the man with one ear, but Daddy and I came up with this recipe in his honor. Note that you'll need one week for the cherries to soak in the moonshine.

1 10-ounce jar maraschino cherries

1 cup clear moonshine (or bourbon)

1 tablespoon fresh lime juice

1 tablespoon fresh orange juice

MOONSHINE-SOAKED CHERRIES

∴ **MAKES ONE 10-OUNCE JAR**

1   Drain the cherries, reserving the juice.

2   Pour the moonshine over the cherries. Let soak for 1 week in the refrigerator, in the jar they came in, covered with the lid.

3   In a small saucepan set over medium-high heat, cook the reserved cherry juice until it has reduced by half, 10 to 12 minutes. Stir in the lime juice and orange juice. Store, covered, in the refrigerator until ready to use with the moonshine-soaked cherries.

4   After the week is up, drain the moonshine from the cherries. Add half of the moonshine back to the cherries and fill the remainder of the jar with the cherry-juice reduction. The cherries will keep in an airtight container in the refrigerator for 1 month.

No bowl of ice cream is complete without a spoonful or two of wet nuts. Here, I use walnuts, but you can also use pecans, cashews, or peanuts. This recipe doubles easily and can be made in 4-ounce glass jars to give as gifts for the holidays.

1 cup light corn syrup

¼ cup maple syrup

¼ cup (packed) light brown sugar

2 cups coarsely chopped walnuts

WET WALNUTS

·⋮· **MAKES 3 CUPS**

In a medium saucepan set over medium heat, combine the corn syrup, maple syrup, brown sugar, and 2 tablespoons water. Bring the mixture to a simmer and cook, stirring occasionally, until slightly thickened, 5 minutes. Remove the pan from the heat and let cool. Stir in the nuts. The nuts will keep in an airtight container in the refrigerator for 1 month.

Make sure you have uninterrupted time before starting this recipe. It can be a little tricky when it comes to cooking the sugar in the cast-iron skillet. If you love caramel as much as I do, however, I feel certain you will agree it is well worth the time. Take note that the pie needs to chill overnight in the fridge so plan accordingly!

CARAMEL PIE

∴ MAKES ONE 9-INCH DEEP-DISH PIE

8 large eggs, separated and at room temperature (see Hint, page 35)

2 cups plus 1 tablespoon sugar

¼ cup unbleached all-purpose flour, sifted

½ cup (1 stick) unsalted butter

2 cups half-and-half, at room temperature

2 teaspoons vanilla extract

1 baked 9-inch deep-dish Basic Piecrust (page 150) or Cookie Crust (page 154)

1   In the bowl of a stand mixer fitted with the whisk attachment, beat the egg yolks on high speed until pale, 3 minutes. Add 1 cup of the sugar and the flour, and beat just to combine. Scrape down the sides and around the bottom of the bowl. Increase the speed to high for 1 minute.

2   In a medium heavy-bottomed saucepan set over low heat, melt the butter. Whisk in the half-and-half and the egg mixture until completely smooth. Increase the heat to medium and cook, whisking constantly, until the mixture has a custard-like consistency, 15 to 18 minutes. Remove the pan from the heat and press plastic wrap directly onto the custard to prevent a thick skin from forming (remove before adding the caramel).

3   Put 1 cup sugar in a 12-inch cast-iron skillet (or a lighter-colored skillet if you're new to caramel making) set over medium-low heat. As the sugar begins to melt, use a heatproof spatula to carefully and gradually incorporate the unmelted sugar a little at a time; do not stir constantly. When the sugar has reached a light amber color, or 342°F on a candy thermometer (you can carefully tilt the pan to pool the sugar to get a better read on the thermometer) about 20 minutes, add the caramel to the custard and cook, whisking constantly over medium heat until thickened, 8 to 10 minutes. Remove the pan from the heat and add the vanilla. Pour the mixture into the baked piecrust and cool 15 minutes.

4   Preheat the oven to 350°F.

5   In the washed and dried bowl of a stand mixer fitted with the whisk attachment, beat the reserved egg whites with the remaining 1 tablespoon of granulated sugar on high speed until stiff peaks form, 3 to 4 minutes. Spread the meringue over the caramel custard.

6   Bake until the meringue is lightly browned, 10 to 12 minutes. Chill overnight, then slice and serve.

NOTE: Refrigerating baked meringue will produce little beads of syrup on the meringue. This will not affect the taste.

If you've ever picked strawberries yourself, you know what it means to be greedy. Even though I start with two buckets, certain they'll hold enough strawberries to satisfy my excitement, I always find that I pack them full and still gaze longingly over the continuous rows of stunning berries in the fields. Gorgeous, perfectly ripe fruit makes this pie sing.

GRACIOUS PLENTY STRAWBERRY PIE

∴ MAKES ONE 12 × 18-INCH PIE

1 Lightly grease a 12 × 18-inch half-sheet pan using butter, shortening, or Pan Grease (page 16). On a lightly floured surface, knead together and roll 3 recipes of the dough out into a 14 × 20-inch rectangle. Carefully roll the dough around the rolling pin and unroll it onto the prepared pan. Press the dough into the edges and corners, being careful not to tear it. Leave any overhanging dough.

2 Roll out the remaining dough into a 12 × 18-inch rectangle. You will use this later to cover the top of the pie.

3 Preheat the oven to 350°F.

4 In a large bowl, combine the strawberries, lemon juice, and both extracts. In a small bowl, combine the sugar and cornstarch, and carefully toss the mixture with the strawberries so as not to smash the strawberries. Pour the filling onto the prepared dough and spread evenly. Top with the remaining dough, seal the edges by pressing them together with a fork, trim any overhanging dough, and cut four or five slits in the top to allow the steam to vent. Brush the crust with some water and then sprinkle with sugar.

5 Bake until the crust is golden brown and the strawberries are bubbling, 50 to 60 minutes. Serve warm or at room temperature.

Butter or shortening or Pan Grease (page 16)

Unbleached all-purpose flour, for rolling

5 recipes Almond Piecrust (page 157) or Basic Piecrust (page 150)

FILLING

8 cups sliced fresh strawberries

2 tablespoons fresh lemon juice

1 teaspoon vanilla extract

½ teaspoon almond extract

1 cup sugar, plus more for sprinkling

2 tablespoons cornstarch

For the best fresh coconut taste, I always steep the frozen coconut before adding it to the other ingredients. It flavors the custard nicely and gives the pie a rice-pudding-like consistency that I love.

COCONUT CREAM PIE

⠐⠆ **MAKES ONE 9-INCH DEEP-DISH PIE**

1 Preheat the oven to 350°F.

2 In a 2-quart heavy-bottomed saucepan set over medium-high heat, bring 1 cup of the cream and the coconut milk to a low boil. Turn off the heat, stir in the salt and thawed coconut, cover, and steep for 30 minutes.

3 In the bowl of a stand mixer fitted with the whisk attachment, beat the eggs and granulated sugar on high speed until light, 3 minutes. With the mixer on low, slowly add the warm coconut-milk mixture. Scrape down the sides and around the bottom of the bowl. Add the sweetened coconut flakes and vanilla and coconut extracts. Beat on low for 1 minute. Pour the filling into the prepared crust.

4 Bake until the pie is firm, 45 to 55 minutes. Cool completely and then refrigerate for 4 hours or overnight.

5 In the chilled bowl of a stand mixer, beat the remaining 1 cup cream and the confectioners' sugar on high speed until stiff peaks form, 3 to 4 minutes. Spread the whipped cream over the cold pie and garnish with the toasted coconut flakes.

> **HINT** To toast coconut: Spread the sweetened coconut evenly on a sheet pan. Bake at 350°F until browned just around the edges, 7 minutes. Stir and bake until golden, 3 to 4 minutes.

Variation

CRUSTLESS COCONUT CREAM PIE This is also delicious made without the crust. Pour the prepared filling into a lightly greased 2-quart glass baking dish. Bake at 350°F until firm, 45 to 55 minutes. You'll still want to spread the whipped cream over the pie and sprinkle with the toasted coconut flakes.

2 cups heavy whipping cream, divided

1 cup canned coconut milk

Pinch of salt

2 6-ounce packages frozen fresh coconut, thawed

4 large eggs

¾ cup granulated sugar

1 cup sweetened coconut flakes

1 teaspoon vanilla extract

1 teaspoon coconut extract

1 baked 9-inch deep dish Basic Piecrust (page 150)

2 tablespoons confectioners' sugar

½ to ¾ cup large-flake unsweetened coconut, toasted (see Hint), for garnish

My family absolutely loves to dip pretzels into mint chocolate-chip ice cream! So, I turned that idea into a pie. This salty, creamy, minty chocolate pie is the best of both worlds—and it doesn't melt.

MINT CHOCOLATE LAYER PIE
with a pretzel crust

∴ **MAKES ONE 9-INCH SPRINGFORM PIE**

1   **Make the crust:** Grease the bottom and sides of a 9-inch spring-form pan with butter or nonstick cooking spray. In a medium bowl, combine the graham cracker crumbs and pretzels. Add the melted butter and mix well to moisten. Press into the bottom and ½ inch up the sides of the prepared pan.

2   Pour 2 cups of the ganache over the crust, spreading evenly to cover the surface.

3   **Prepare the filling:** In a 2-quart saucepan set over medium heat, whisk together the sugar and cream until the sugar is dissolved. Remove from the heat. Add the chocolate chips and let sit until melted, 5 minutes. Whisk until smooth.

4   In a medium bowl, whisk the egg yolks. Slowly drizzle in ½ cup of the melted chocolate mixture, whisking constantly so as not to cook and scramble the yolks. Pour the yolk mixture into the remaining chocolate mixture and return to cooking over medium heat until thickened, 6 to 8 minutes. Remove the pan from the heat and stir in the mint extract. Let cool slightly, 15 to 20 minutes, before pouring the filling into the crust.

5   Drizzle 1 to 1½ cups ganache over the chocolate filling. Refrigerate at least 4 hours or overnight. Remove the sides of the pan and garnish with additional pretzel pieces, if desired. The pie will keep in the refrigerator for 1 week. Keep covered.

PRETZEL CRUST

Butter or nonstick cooking spray

1 cup graham cracker crumbs

1 cup crushed pretzels, plus more pieces for garnish (optional)

½ cup (1 stick) unsalted butter, melted

Chocolate Ganache (page 132), made with white chocolate

FILLING

1 cup sugar

½ cup heavy whipping cream

1 cup semisweet chocolate chips

4 large egg yolks

2 teaspoons mint extract

Back during my college days, my friends and I rarely went anywhere without someone ordering a pitcher of Long Island Iced Tea. It was a far cry from any iced tea my mother ever made but quite tasty (among other things). This pie is bound to bring back a few memories if you had a wild and crazy spring break or two!

LONG ISLAND ICED TEA PIE

∴ **MAKE ONE 9-INCH DEEP-DISH PIE**

1 Preheat the oven to 350°F.

2 Put the boiling water and teabag in a glass measuring cup, cover, and let steep for 5 minutes.

3 In the bowl of a stand mixer fitted with the whisk attachment, beat the butter and sugar on high speed until light and fluffy, 3 minutes. Beat in the egg yolks for 1 minute. Scrape down the sides and around the bottom of the bowl. Beat for 30 more seconds. Add the lemon zest, lemon juice, flour, and salt, along with all four of the liquors and 1 cup of the tea. Beat on low speed to combine, 1 minute.

4 Sprinkle the cornmeal evenly over the unbaked piecrust. Pour in the pie filling.

5 Bake until the pie is set and firm, 55 to 60 minutes. Refrigerate 3 to 4 hours or overnight. Serve cold.

1 cup boiling water

1 family-size tea bag

1 cup (2 sticks) unsalted butter, at room temperature

2 cups sugar

8 large egg yolks

2 teaspoons grated lemon zest

2 tablespoons fresh lemon juice

¼ cup unbleached all-purpose flour, sifted

¼ teaspoon salt

2 teaspoons dark rum

2 teaspoons vodka

2 teaspoons gin

2 teaspoons tequila

1 teaspoon cornmeal

1 unbaked Basic Piecrust (page 150), fitted into a deep-dish 9-inch pie plate

This is a perfect dessert to make when there is a big group to serve. The apples and the pecan streusel, all baked together, make this a perfect crowd-pleaser—and I find it often feeds up to 48 people if I cut it into 2-inch pieces. Who among us doesn't love a nice slice of apple pie? It will make you the star of the show, with oohs and aahs galore!

GRACIOUS PLENTY APPLE PIE with pecan streusel

∴ **MAKES ONE 12 × 18-INCH PIE**

1 Lightly grease a 12 × 18-inch half-sheet pan with butter, shortening, or Pan Grease (page 16). On a lightly floured surface, knead together the batches of dough and roll the dough out into a 14 × 20-inch rectangle. Carefully roll the dough around the rolling pin and unroll it onto the prepared pan. Press the dough into the edges and corners, being careful not to tear it. Trim any overhang and set aside.

2 **Make the topping:** In a large bowl, using your fingers or a whisk, combine the butter, sugar, and flour; it will be lumpy. Stir in the pecans.

3 Preheat the oven to 350°F.

4 **Prepare the filling:** In a large bowl, toss the sliced apples with the lemon juice and set aside.

5 In a medium bowl, combine both sugars, the flour, and cinnamon. Sprinkle it over the apples, toss with a spatula to combine, and carefully arrange the apples over the unbaked pie dough. Evenly sprinkle the topping over the apples.

6 Bake until the apples are tender and bubbly, 1 hour. Serve warm or at room temperature.

Butter or shortening or Pan Grease (page 16)

3 recipes Basic Piecrust (page 150) or Southern Piecrust (page 152)

PECAN STREUSEL TOPPING

1 cup (2 sticks) unsalted butter, at room temperature

¾ cup (packed) light brown sugar

½ cup unbleached all-purpose flour

4 cups chopped pecans

FILLING

12 large apples, such as Winesap or Rome Beauty, peeled, cored, and thinly sliced

2 tablespoons fresh lemon juice

1 cup (packed) light brown sugar

½ cup granulated sugar

¼ cup unbleached all-purpose flour

1 teaspoon ground cinnamon

These fritters make me think of two of my favorite things: beignets and hush puppies. Like both of them, you'll want to fry these fritters until perfectly brown and eat them hot, right out of the fryer. You might want to give them a few minutes to cool off just a bit so you don't burn your mouth—though it's hard to wait! I love these apple fritters because they are crispy on the outside and so light and moist on the inside. They also make your kitchen smell really good while you're frying them!

APPLE FRITTERS

·⁝· **MAKES THIRTY 2-INCH FRITTERS**

2 cups unbleached all-purpose flour

2 tablespoons granulated sugar

2 teaspoons baking powder

½ teaspoon ground cinnamon

1 teaspoon salt

1 cup whole milk

1 large egg

1 teaspoon vanilla extract

2 cups peeled and coarsely chopped apples, about 4 medium

2 quarts vegetable oil, for frying

Confectioners' sugar, for dusting

1 In a medium bowl, sift together the flour, granulated sugar, baking powder, cinnamon, and salt.

2 In a large bowl, whisk together the milk, egg, and vanilla. Fold in the flour mixture just until combined. Fold in the apples until well coated.

3 In a large heavy-bottomed frying pan set over medium-high heat, heat 1½ inches of oil until it reads 375°F on an instant-read thermometer. Working in batches, drop the coated apples by rounded tablespoonfuls into the hot oil and cook until browned all over, 3 to 4 minutes per side. Transfer to a paper-towel-lined plate to drain. Dust with confectioners' sugar and serve warm.

Variation

PECAN FRITTERS Substitute 3 cups of coarsely chopped pecans in place of the apples.

If you don't need as big a dessert as the Mississippi Mud Cake (page 42) but still want the delicious taste, make this pie instead. You probably have all of the ingredients on hand. It's an easy make-ahead dessert, too.

MISSISSIPPI MUD PIE

∴ MAKE ONE 9-INCH PIE

1 Combine the cold water and coffee in a small bowl, and sprinkle the gelatin over the top. Let sit for 5 minutes.

2 In a medium heavy-bottomed saucepan set over medium heat, combine the chocolate chips, sugar, and ½ cup of cream, whisking until the chips have melted and the mixture is smooth, 6 minutes. Whisk in the dissolved gelatin. Pour the filling into the piecrust. Top with the toasted pecans. Refrigerate until set, at least 3 hours or overnight.

3 In the chilled bowl of a stand mixer fitted with the chilled whisk attachment, beat the remaining cup of cream and confectioners' sugar on high speed until stiff peaks form, 3 to 4 minutes. Spread the whipped cream over the chilled pie and drizzle with chocolate syrup. Serve cold. This pie is best enjoyed within a day or two. Keep it refrigerated and covered.

Variation

Instead of the whipping cream, top the toasted pecans with mini marshmallows and drizzle with chocolate syrup.

2 tablespoons cold water

3 tablespoons cold, strong coffee

1 tablespoon unflavored gelatin

½ cup semisweet chocolate chips

½ cup granulated sugar

1½ cups heavy whipping cream

1 baked 9-inch Sweet Piecrust (page 156) or Chocolate Piecrust (page 153)

1 cup chopped pecans, toasted (see Hint, page 42)

1 cup heavy whipping cream

2 tablespoons confectioners' sugar

Chocolate syrup, for drizzling

One summer many years ago, I was invited to a small, local orchard to pick peaches. My mother and I loaded up a few clothes baskets, hopped into Daddy's truck, and headed out. Though it was very hot and humid—and I was seven months pregnant—we stood in the back of the truck and picked peaches to our hearts' content. We made quite a few peach desserts over the next week or so, especially this one.

GRACIOUS PLENTY PEACH PIE

·⁖· MAKES ONE 12 × 18-INCH PIE

1 Lightly grease a 12 × 18-inch half-sheet pan using butter, shortening, or Pan Grease (page 16). On a lightly floured surface, knead together 2 recipes (half of the dough) and roll the dough out into a 14 × 20-inch rectangle (leave the rest of the dough in the refrigerator). Carefully roll the dough around the rolling pin and unroll it onto the prepared pan. Press the dough into the edges and corners, being careful not to tear it. Leave any overhanging dough.

2 Preheat the oven to 350°F.

3 In a large heavy-bottomed skillet set over medium heat, melt the butter. Whisk in the brown sugar and flour, and cook just until smooth, 5 minutes. Remove the pan from the heat and whisk in the rum and cinnamon, if using. Put the peaches in a bowl and toss with the rum mixture. Pour the filling onto the prepared crust.

4 Roll the remaining dough into a 14 × 20-inch rectangle. Carefully roll the dough around the rolling pin and unroll it over the filling. Trim any overhanging dough, and press the edges together with a fork to seal. Cut four or five slits in the top.

5 Bake until the crust is golden brown and the peaches are bubbling, 60 to 65 minutes. Serve warm or at room temperature.

Variations

You can use the same amount of dough as in the Gracious Plenty Apple Pie with Pecan Streusel (page 182) and top with the streusel.

Butter or shortening or Pan Grease (page 16)

4 recipes Basic Piecrust (page 150)

Unbleached all-purpose flour, for rolling

FILLING

½ cup (1 stick) unsalted butter

2 cups (packed) light brown sugar

½ cup unbleached all-purpose flour

½ cup dark rum

½ to 1 teaspoon ground cinnamon (optional)

16 large, ripe peaches, peeled, pitted, and thinly sliced

There is one dessert that will always be at the top of the list as my ultimate comfort-food dessert: Mama Bishop's rice pudding. Well, these rice fritters are like that pudding on steroids! They are dense, with a rich custard-like texture on the inside. The citrus flavors, along with a surprise bite into a hidden golden raisin, make these fritters a fun and fancy finger-food dessert. They do take a while to make, so be sure to give yourself plenty of time. You may want to pour yourself a glass or two of Marsala to enjoy while you're cooking the fritters.

RICE FRITTERS

∴ **MAKES 3 DOZEN**

2 cups uncooked long grain white rice

2 cups whole milk

1 medium orange, sliced

1 lemon, sliced

2¼ cups sugar

1⅓ cups golden raisins

¼ cup good-quality Marsala

1 heaping tablespoon unbleached all-purpose flour

3 large eggs

2 large egg yolks

Pinch of baking powder

Pinch of salt

1 quart vegetable oil, for frying

1   In an 8-quart heavy-bottomed saucepan set over low heat, combine the rice, 2¼ cups of the water, the milk, and orange and lemon slices. Cook, stirring constantly with a wooden spoon, until most of the liquid is absorbed, 20 minutes. Add 1½ cups of the sugar, increase the heat to medium-low, and continue cooking, stirring constantly, until thick and creamy, 20 minutes. Stir in the raisins and the Marsala. Remove the pan from the heat and let cool for 30 to 40 minutes. Remove the orange and lemon slices; discard.

2   In a small bowl, beat together the flour, eggs, egg yolks, baking powder, and salt. Add to the cooled rice mixture, stirring vigorously until well blended. Spread rice mixture evenly onto a rimmed baking sheet and chill, uncovered, for 1 hour before frying.

3   Heat the oil in a large pot set over medium-high heat until an instant-read thermometer registers 350°F. Test the temperature by dropping a spoonful of batter into the oil; if the batter sizzles and rises quickly to the top, the oil is ready.

4   Working in batches, drop heaping tablespoons of batter (you can also use a 1-ounce scoop) into the hot oil. Do not overcrowd the pan. Fry until browned evenly all over, 5 to 7 minutes per side. Transfer to a paper-towel-lined plate to drain. Roll the fritters in the remaining ¾ cup sugar. Serve hot.

A friend who is a wonderful cook never seems to go to a lot of trouble, and yet everything she makes is really delicious. She gave me this simple recipe for my book, since it is one of my personal favorites. It's an ideal summertime dessert because you don't even need to use the stove. Also, it includes my weakness: sweetened condensed milk. I've never opened a can of it and not eaten several spoonfuls before making the recipe!

1 14-ounce can sweetened condensed milk

⅓ cup fresh lime juice

2 to 4 tablespoons good-quality tequila

2 tablespoons good-quality orange liqueur

1 cup heavy whipping cream

2 tablespoons confectioners' sugar

Pretzel Crust (page 180)

MARGARITA PIE

∴ **MAKES ONE 9-INCH SPRINGFORM PIE**

1   In a medium bowl, whisk together the condensed milk, lime juice, tequila, and orange liqueur.

2   In the chilled bowl of a stand mixer fitted with the whisk attachment, beat the cream and confectioners' sugar on high speed until stiff peaks form, 3 to 4 minutes. Fold it into the condensed milk mixture, being careful not to overmix. Pour the filling into the prepared crust, cover, and freeze for at least 4 hours or overnight. Remove the springform sides before serving.

Variation

LEMON MARGARITA PIE   For a light and refreshing pie at Thanksgiving or Christmas, use fresh lemon juice in place of the lime juice, along with ½ teaspoon lemon extract. Pour the lemon filling into a gingerbread piecrust (see Variations, page 95). Garnish with a few Gingerbread Cookies (page 93).

When I want to serve an old-timey favorite from the Bishops who lived over on Lover's Lane, I serve fried applesauce pies. Lucy Bishop, another great-aunt and another great cook in the family, always made the absolute best ones ever! I believe the secret was in her dough. She was very careful not to overwork it so that it wasn't tough. Of course, she made her dough by hand, and not in a food processor. Fried pies are fun because they can be filled with all sorts of yummy things. Find a few of my favorite fillings on page 195.

2¾ cups self-rising flour

2 tablespoons granulated sugar

¼ cup vegetable shortening, cold

¼ cup (½ stick) unsalted butter, cold

1 large egg yolk

½ to ¾ cup ice water

Filling of your choice (recipes follow)

2 cups vegetable oil, for frying

Confectioners' sugar or granulated sugar, for dusting

FRIED PIES

· ⫶ · MAKES TWELVE 6-INCH PIES

1 In the bowl of a food processor fitted with the blade attachment, blend together 2 cups of the flour and the granulated sugar. Add the shortening and butter, and pulse several times until the mixture has a cornmeal-like consistency. Blend in the egg yolk just to combine. With the processor running, gradually add the ice water, a little at a time, just until the dough forms a ball.

2 Using the remaining ¾ cup flour, flour the work surface, rolling pin, and your hands before removing the dough from the processor. Working in two batches, roll out the dough until it is ⅛ to ¼ inch thick. Using a biscuit cutter, cut out twelve 6-inch circles. Place 2 heaping tablespoons of cooled filling into the center of each circle. Using your fingertips, wet the edges with water, fold the dough over so the pies are half-moons, and seal them by pressing with the tines of a fork. Lightly sprinkle the pies with flour and refrigerate for at least 45 minutes.

3 In a large skillet with deep sides, heat 1 inch of oil over medium-high heat until it reads 375°F on an instant-read thermometer. Working in batches, fry the pies until golden brown, 3 minutes. Flip the pies and fry until the second side is golden brown, 1 to 2 more minutes. Transfer to a paper-towel-lined plate to drain. Dust with sugar. Serve warm.

HINT This recipe doubles easily and can be made into smaller or larger pies depending on the size you want to make.

recipe continues

This applesauce is delicious all by itself or even spooned on a slice of Miss Daisy's Plain Pound Cake (page 31). I sometimes omit the cinnamon and vanilla and substitute freshly ground black pepper. Also, add 1 cup of shredded extra-sharp Cheddar cheese to the apple mixture just before filling and frying the pies for a delicious variation. I omit the cinnamon but not the vanilla when adding the cheese.

APPLESAUCE FILLING

⋰ **MAKES 3 CUPS**

½ cup (1 stick) unsalted butter

¼ cup granulated sugar

3 Granny Smith apples, peeled, cored, and sliced (about 3 cups)

2 tablespoons light brown sugar

½ teaspoon ground cinnamon

¼ teaspoon vanilla extract

In a large skillet set over medium heat, melt the butter with the granulated sugar. Add the apples, cover, and simmer until cooked and coming apart, 15 to 20 minutes. Remove the pan from the heat and stir in the brown sugar, cinnamon, and vanilla. Let cool completely before using.

This filling can also be used between cake layers, as a spread on toast or bagels, or over ice cream.

STRAWBERRY FILLING

⋰ **MAKES 3 CUPS**

4 cups hulled and sliced strawberries

½ cup sugar

¼ cup (½ stick) unsalted butter

1 teaspoon vanilla extract

¼ teaspoon almond extract (optional)

1 In a medium bowl, combine the strawberries and sugar. Let stand at room temperature for 30 minutes. Drain, reserving 2 tablespoons of the juice.

2 In a large skillet set over medium heat, melt the butter. Add the strawberries and the reserved strawberry juice. Increase the heat to medium-high and cook, stirring constantly, until most of the liquid has evaporated, 18 minutes. Remove the pan from the heat. Add the vanilla and almond extract, if desired, and let cool completely before using.

recipe continues

There are two things I can never have too much of: peaches and pecans. This peach filling is as versatile as the strawberry one on page 195. You're limited only by your imagination. Make sure your peaches are perfectly ripe but not overly so, or they will be mushy after frying.

PEACH FILLING

· ∴ · **MAKES 3 CUPS**

5 ripe peaches, peeled, pitted and chopped into ½-inch pieces (about 3 cups)

¼ cup sugar

½ teaspoon vanilla extract

Sprinkle of ground cinnamon (optional)

In a medium bowl, combine the peaches and sugar. Let stand at room temperature for 30 minutes. Drain well. Stir in the vanilla and cinnamon, if using.

Where I live in the beautiful Upstate of South Carolina, the best blueberries come in around the Fourth of July. These freshly picked berries are easy to keep in the freezer and then bring a nice warm taste of summer when made into fried pies on a cold winter day.

BLUEBERRY FILLING

· ∴ · **MAKES 3 CUPS**

4 cups ripe, plump blueberries

½ cup sugar

1 tablespoon cornstarch

2 tablespoons fresh lemon juice

¼ cup (½ stick) unsalted butter

1 teaspoon vanilla extract

1   In the bowl of a food processor fitted with the blade attachment, pulse the blueberries with the sugar until coarsely chopped. Let sit at room temperature for 30 minutes.

2   In a small bowl, dissolve the cornstarch in the lemon juice.

3   In a large skillet set over medium heat, melt the butter. Stir in the blueberry mixture and then the cornstarch mixture. Increase the heat to medium-high, bring to a low boil, and cook, stirring constantly, until thickened, 6 to 8 minutes. Remove the pan from the heat. Stir in the vanilla. Let cool completely before using or freezing.

ICE CREAMS
and
puddings

One of my most vivid summertime memories is watching Aunt Daisy's husband, Jamie, in his overalls, sitting on an old milk crate and churning ice cream. It was no easy feat, as this was back in the day when ice cream had to be churned *by hand,* using a handle that looked more like a crank.

On Sunday afternoons when company came calling, they were the ones who felt extra special if it was an ice-cream-making Sunday. Fresh peach ice cream was a favorite of everyone, except me. I loved vanilla with a very heavy pour of canned Hershey's syrup. It melted in a hurry on a hot summer day, so you had to eat it that way, too. Brain freeze!

Thank goodness, we have electric ice cream churns these days that will make a batch in half the time it took my Uncle Jamie to crank one out. It's a good thing, too, that all things ice cream related are easy to order and have delivered in only a few days. That's what I did. I ordered a 6-quart churn, since I'm wired into that "gracious plenty" mode. After all, while you're at it, you might as well make a lot instead of just a little, right?

> **HINT** Please keep in mind that ice cream bases (and many ice cream bowls) need to be refrigerated (or frozen) the night before you plan on churning the ice cream. Each of the ice cream recipes requires a 6-quart ice cream churn. The recipes can be easily adjusted and quantities reduced to fit a smaller electric churn, whether you have a counter model or just don't want to make as much.

· ⋮ ·

I love ice cream! I love lemon! I especially love putting the two of them together in a big ice cream churn. The result is a bright, fresh, tart burst of flavor all mixed together in a rich, creamy texture. What makes this ice cream sing is the lemon curd. One spoonful will wake your taste buds right up and is guaranteed to even make you pucker a little, too. That said, the ice cream is delicate and delicious without the extra lemon curd addition, too.

LEMON CURD ICE CREAM

∴ **MAKES 4 QUARTS**

24 large egg yolks

6 cups heavy whipping cream

4 cups whole milk

3 cups sugar

2 cups fresh lemon juice (16 to 20 lemons)

1 teaspoon salt

½ cup grated lemon zest

2 tablespoons lemon extract

1 tablespoon vanilla extract

4 cups Lemon Curd (page 145, optional)

1   In an 8-quart heavy-bottomed saucepan, whisk the egg yolks until smooth. Add the cream, milk, sugar, lemon juice, and salt and set the pan over medium heat. Cook, whisking constantly, until the sugar dissolves, 5 minutes. Increase the heat slightly. Cook, whisking constantly, with the whisk always maintaining contact with the bottom of the pan, until the mixture is slightly thickened and registers 170°F on a candy thermometer, 12 to 14 minutes. Remove the pan from the heat. Whisk in the lemon zest, lemon extract, and the vanilla. Let cool. Cover and refrigerate overnight.

2   Churn the base in an ice cream machine according to the manufacturer's instructions. Fold in the lemon curd, if using. Transfer to a freezer-safe container and freeze until hard.

HINT Both pint and quart ice cream containers work and are readily available online.

NOTE: All of the recipes for ice cream can be reduced by half or three-quarters to make a smaller batch. But I figure, hey, while I'm at it, I might as well make a gracious plenty!

Not every dessert needs to be the star of the show. If you ask me, there is always room for something plain and simple. Old-fashioned vanilla ice cream is a much-loved treat. Around my house, we sometimes save a little room in each bowl for some Chocolate Sauce (page 138), too. You can also mix in some yummy things, if you like: after churning and before freezing, fold in 4 cups of fresh fruit pieces, caramel-coated popcorn, chocolate-covered peanuts or raisins, or your cookie pieces of choice.

32 large egg yolks

10 cups whole milk

6 cups heavy whipping cream

4½ cups sugar

1 teaspoon salt

2 tablespoons vanilla paste

2 tablespoons vanilla extract

VANILLA ICE CREAM

∴ **MAKES 5 QUARTS**

1   In an 8-quart heavy-bottomed saucepan, whisk the egg yolks until smooth. Set the pan over medium heat and add the milk, cream, sugar, and salt. Cook, whisking constantly, until the sugar dissolves, 5 minutes. Increase the heat slightly. Cook, whisking constantly, with the whisk always maintaining contact with the bottom of the pan, until the mixture is slightly thickened and registers 170°F on a candy thermometer, 12 to 14 minutes. Remove the pan from the heat. Whisk in the vanilla paste and vanilla extract. Let cool. Cover and refrigerate overnight.

2   Churn the base in an ice cream machine according to the manu-facturer's instructions. Transfer to a freezer-safe container and freeze until hard.

Variations

STRAWBERRY ALMOND Substitute 1 cup almond paste for the vanilla paste. In addition, add 1 tablespoon almond extract along with the vanilla after removing the custard from the heat. After churning, fold in 6 cups sliced ripe strawberries.

CHERRY Add 1 tablespoon cherry extract along with the vanilla. After churning, fold in 6 cups pitted coarsely chopped fresh cherries.

RUM RAISIN Soak 4 cups raisins in 1 cup spiced rum overnight. Add the raisin mixture, rum and all, to the custard before churning. For a stronger rum flavor, add 1 tablespoon rum extract along with the vanilla extract.

PEANUT BUTTER After churning, fold in 3 to 4 cups peanut butter. Both smooth and crunchy are delicious, so use your favorite.

I like to keep a quart or two of this sinful ice cream in my freezer for when I need a fix. Just a spoonful or two is all it takes for me to start feeling perkier and grinning ear to ear. Pack and freeze it in pint containers, and you'll have plenty to share with your friends—as well as your own personal pint so you can eat it right out of the carton. It's also good with a couple of sturdy, rippled potato chips on the side for dipping instead of using a spoon! There are so many options to add to this ice cream before freezing it in containers. Broken pieces of your favorite candy bars are delicious, as are swirls of Chocolate Ganache (page 132), toasted nuts, Moonshine-Soaked Cherries (page 172), or use the ice cream to make ice cream sandwiches with cookies (page 96). The possibilities are endless!

32 large egg yolks

2 scant cups Dutch-processed cocoa powder

12 cups whole milk

4 cups heavy whipping cream

4½ cups sugar

½ teaspoon salt

¼ cup vanilla extract

¼ cup espresso powder (optional)

CHOCOLATE ICE CREAM

· ⁖ · MAKES 5 QUARTS

1   In an 8-quart heavy-bottomed saucepan, whisk the egg yolks and cocoa powder with 2 cups of the whole milk until smooth and paste-like. Whisk in the remaining milk, cream, sugar, and salt until smooth. Set the pan over medium heat and cook, whisking occasionally, until the sugar is dissolved, 5 minutes. Increase the heat slightly and cook, stirring constantly with the whisk always maintaining contact with the bottom of the saucepan, until the mixture is thickened and registers 170°F to 175°F on a candy thermometer, 12 to 14 minutes. Remove the pan from the heat. Whisk in the vanilla and the espresso powder, if using. Let cool. Cover and refrigerate overnight.

2   Churn the base in an ice cream machine according to the manufacturer's instructions. Transfer to a freezer-safe container and freeze until hard.

When I want to fold some roasted fruit into my ice cream, I prefer to use this recipe instead of the Vanilla Ice Cream (page 202). It is richer and has more depth of flavor, which helps it stand up to the bold fruit. I've given three of my favorite roasted-fruit mix-ins, so you can experiment.

ICE CREAM
with roasted fruit

⁞ MAKES 4 QUARTS

6 cups heavy whipping cream

6 cups half-and-half

2 cups granulated sugar

1 cup (packed) dark brown sugar

1 teaspoon salt

2 tablespoons fresh lemon juice

1 tablespoon vanilla paste

1 tablespoon vanilla extract

1 tablespoon banana, peach, or pineapple extract (match the flavor to whatever roasted fruit you plan to use; optional)

4 cups Roasted Fruit of your choice (recipes follow)

1 In an 8-quart heavy-bottomed saucepan set over medium-high heat, combine the heavy cream, half-and-half, both sugars, and salt. Cook, whisking, until the sugar dissolves, 5 minutes. Bring to a low boil. Remove the pan from the heat and whisk in the lemon juice, vanilla paste, vanilla extract, and the fruit extract, if using. Refrigerate for 1 hour, then stir in the roasted fruit. Cover and refrigerate overnight.

2 Churn the base in an ice cream machine according to the manu-facturer's instructions. Transfer to a freezer-safe container and freeze until hard.

ROASTED PINEAPPLE

⁞ MAKES 4 CUPS

½ cup (1 stick) unsalted butter, melted

2 16-ounce cans sliced pineapple in its own juice, drained

½ cup (packed) dark brown sugar

1 Preheat the oven to 400°F. Line a rimmed baking sheet with foil and brush with 2 tablespoons of the melted butter.

2 Arrange the pineapple slices in a single layer on the prepared baking sheet. Sprinkle evenly with the brown sugar and drizzle with the remaining butter. Bake until they turn deep golden brown, 20 minutes. Let cool completely and cut into ½-inch pieces before adding them to the ice cream base.

recipe continues

ROASTED BANANAS

·⦂· **MAKES 4 CUPS**

1   Preheat the oven to 400°F. Line a rimmed baking sheet with foil and brush with 2 tablespoons of the melted butter.

2   Working in batches of 5 bananas at a time, split the bananas lengthwise and arrange them on the prepared baking sheet, cut side down. Brush each banana with melted butter and sprinkle with brown sugar. Bake until golden brown, 15 minutes. Remove from the oven and let cool. Continue with the remaining bananas. Let cool completely and slice before adding them to the ice cream base.

½ cup (1 stick) unsalted butter, melted and cooled slightly

10 medium ripe bananas, peeled, with few or no brown spots

1 cup (packed) dark brown sugar

ROASTED PEACHES

·⦂· **MAKES 4 CUPS**

1   Preheat the oven to 400°F. Line a rimmed baking sheet with foil and brush with 2 tablespoons of the melted butter.

2   In a medium bowl, combine the peaches, sugar, and remaining butter. Arrange them evenly in a single layer on the prepared pan. Bake until they turn deep golden brown, 20 minutes. Let cool completely before adding to the ice cream base.

½ cup (1 stick) unsalted butter, melted

6 cups frozen sliced peaches, thawed and chopped

½ cup (packed) dark brown sugar

When I was a little girl, there were few things I loved more than licking the spoon after my mother made this pudding. I would beg her to leave just a little taste in the pan for me. This recipe doubles easily, so you can make enough for everybody to have an extra spoonful. This pudding is delicious by itself, but I also like to use it as a filling between cake layers.

¾ cup sugar

1 tablespoon self-rising flour

1 12-ounce can evaporated milk

2 large eggs

1 teaspoon vanilla extract

VANILLA PUDDING

·⠇· MAKE 1¾ CUPS

1 In a 1½-quart heavy-bottomed saucepan, whisk together the sugar and flour. Whisk in the evaporated milk and eggs until smooth. Set the pan over medium heat and cook, stirring constantly, until thickened, 10 to 12 minutes. Remove the pan from the heat. Whisk in the vanilla.

2 Pour the pudding into a bowl and cover with plastic wrap, making sure that the plastic touches the entire surface of the pudding to prevent a thick, rubbery film from forming. Refrigerate until cold, at least 3 hours or overnight.

I love serving this custard in my mother's parfait dishes, decorated with a few Gingerbread Cookies (page 93) standing at attention along the sides. I'm also partial to a Moonshine-Soaked Cherry (page 172) or two on top for when I'm having a few of my girlfriends over during the holidays. Try using the custard as a filling between cake layers or in the gingerbread piecrust (see Variations, page 95).

EGGNOG CUSTARD

·∴· MAKES 1¾ CUPS

½ cup sugar

1 tablespoon self-rising flour

1¾ cups store-bought eggnog

2 large eggs

½ teaspoon vanilla extract

½ teaspoon eggnog extract

Freshly grated nutmeg, to taste

1   In a 1½-quart heavy-bottomed saucepan, whisk together the sugar and flour. Whisk in the eggnog and eggs until smooth. Set the pan over medium heat and cook, stirring constantly, until thickened, 10 to 12 minutes. Remove the pan from the heat. Whisk in both extracts and the nutmeg.

2   Pour the custard into a bowl and cover with plastic wrap, making sure that the plastic touches the entire surface of the pudding to prevent a thick, rubbery film from forming. Refrigerate until cold, at least 3 hours or overnight.

Just as it should be, the tangy buttermilk is the star of this ice cream. Delicious all by itself, it's also hard to beat this over a slice of hot-from-the-oven Apple-Walnut Pound Cake (page 32) or Pecan Pie (page 165), or topped with my Peaches Foster (page 142). It's also fun to add some mix-ins: fold in 4 cups of chopped candy, such as Reese's Peanut Butter Cups, turtles, or Butterfingers.

BUTTERMILK ICE CREAM

·⁂· MAKES 2½ QUARTS

12 cups buttermilk

¼ cup cornstarch

6 cups heavy whipping cream

4½ cups sugar

3 tablespoons light corn syrup

2 tablespoons vanilla extract

1   In a medium bowl, whisk together 2 cups of the buttermilk and the cornstarch until smooth. Set aside.

2   In an 8-quart heavy-bottomed saucepan set over medium-high heat, whisk together the remaining 10 cups buttermilk, the cream, sugar, and corn syrup. Cook, whisking, until the sugar dissolves, 2 to 3 minutes. Bring to a boil, then remove the pan from the heat and whisk in the cornstarch mixture.

3   Return the pan to medium-high heat and bring to a low boil, stirring constantly, with the whisk always maintaining contact with the bottom of the pan. Cook until the mixture is thickened, 10 to 12 minutes. Remove the pan from the heat and whisk in the vanilla. Let cool. Cover and refrigerate overnight.

4   Churn the base in an ice cream machine according to the manufacturer's instructions. Transfer to a freezer-safe container and freeze until hard.

Variations

LOW-GLYCEMIC ICE CREAM   Substitute 3 cups agave nectar for the sugar and light corn syrup.

EGGNOG ICE CREAM   Substitute eggnog for the buttermilk, reduce the sugar to 2 cups, and add 2 teaspoons of grated nutmeg. I sometimes mix things up a little and use this in an ice cream pie, with the gingerbread man piecrust (see Variations, page 95) and topped with ½ cup Lemon Curd (page 145).

If I had to pick only one dessert to eat for the rest of my life, this would be it! Doesn't matter what time of year—summertime, wintertime, or anytime in between—the memories this pudding brings and the pure deliciousness of every spoonful always take me to my happy place. It's a wonderful filling for cakes, too, though I often like to lighten it up by folding in 1 cup of Whipped Cream (page 134).

CHOCOLATE PUDDING

·.·. **MAKES 2 CUPS**

1½ cups sugar

½ cup Dutch-processed cocoa powder

¼ cup cornstarch

¼ teaspoon salt

3 large egg yolks

1 14-ounce can evaporated milk

¼ cup (½ stick) unsalted butter, melted

2 teaspoons vanilla extract

1   In a 1½-quart heavy-bottomed saucepan, whisk together the sugar, cocoa, cornstarch, and salt. Whisk in the egg yolks and evaporated milk until smooth. Set the pan over medium-low heat and cook, whisking constantly, until thick and bubbly, 8 to 10 minutes. Remove the pan from the heat and whisk in the butter and vanilla.

2   Pour the pudding into a bowl and cover with plastic wrap, making sure that the plastic touches the entire surface of the pudding to prevent a thick, rubbery film from forming. Refrigerate until cold, at least 3 hours or overnight.

Variation

CHOCOLATE PUDDING FRIED PIES   This pudding is delicious as a filling for Fried Pies (page 193); you will need to double the dough recipe. I also like to add a handful (about ¾ cup) of miniature marshmallows to the cooled chocolate pudding before sealing the pie-dough edges.

A GREAT BIG THANK-YOU

Never in my wildest dreams did I think all of those good times I had as a child—gathering eggs from the chicken pen, making mud pies on the garden bench, and creating a small mess in the kitchen—would lead to all of this. I am forever grateful to everyone who has been a part of this journey with me.

Of course, thanks to Nellie Bishop, Daisy Bishop, and Nervielee Adams Eubanks; the three of you lit the fire by showing me how to do things the best way, the old-fashioned way. I am thankful to my parents, Geraldine and Rock Adams, who were raised by these strong ladies to do things the same way and, even through all of my hard-headedness, didn't let me take the easy way out. I am thankful to my neighbors—the Haithcocks, the Tweedys, and the Seays, who invited me to supper to enjoy their family favorites and share their recipes.

Thank you to chef Louis Osteen for giving me my first glimpse into a real restaurant kitchen and pointing out the "delightfully peppery" taste of watercress and what a difference a little (or a lot) of fresh whipped cream makes on a slice of pie. I love and am so thankful for my friend Sophia Copses Satterfield, who shared her Greek heritage and incredible food knowledge, and who started Oakland House Catering with me after college. Thank you, Stan Baker, for building my first restaurant, As You Like It, just the way I wanted it, and to Gerry Noe, the architect, for your beautiful design.

If it weren't for Rob Greene begging his mom to "please get Miss Kim to teach you how to cook," Cooking Up a Storm never would have happened; I'm so happy you listened, Lee Ann Greene. Thank you to the nearly three hundred students who were a part of that hands-on fun for six years. Being with you each week taught me how eating together as a family and sharing the goodness from our kitchens is all woven into what brings us true joy. It was a blessing to be a part of the energy, love, and laughter. Who would have ever guessed from those four stoves that my love for baking would become a business idea and grow into a nationally recognized cake company that ships my family-recipe cakes to all fifty states!

For my high school and college friend, Danny Graves, I am forever grateful that you took the time to call me nearly thirty years after we graduated to tell me about a television show I should try to get on with my cakes. Thank you to Mindy Zemrak, Clay Newbill and everyone at Sony Pictures and ABC for giving me the opportunity to walk into the tank and pitch my business on the groundbreaking and wildly popular television show *Shark Tank*. Of course, the last seven years would not have been nearly as successful or fun without the investment, business guidance, retreats, and friendship that Barbara Corcoran has given me. To my entire *Shark Tank* family, I love all of you to pieces: Mike Stephens and everyone in the office and the entrepreneurs for always being just a phone call away—Jim Tselikis, Sabin Lomac, Kara Haught, Shelly Hyde, Daniella and Ryan Kelly, Darryl Lenz, Fleetwood Hicks, Jen and Jeff Martin, Trew Quackenbush, Corey Ward, and Melissa and Rick Hinnant—our journey would not be nearly as fun if we hadn't been in it together. Daisy Cakes wouldn't be the company it is today without all the great employees who work hard to bake and ship my family's cake recipes. Thank you for your hard work and dedication. Cheryl Teaster Cooke, you're an office manager extraordinaire and your creative genius never ceases to amaze me! Thank you for always getting it done.

To J. P. Pawliw-Fry, thank you for including me in your book *Performing Under Pressure* and for inviting me to be a part of your presentation at Penguin Random House in New York City. To Maya Mavjee and your entire team, thank you for whisking me away to your conference room after that presentation and spending an hour with me talking about a dessert cookbook. I felt a connection right away. Thank you to Ashley Phillips Meyer, Raquel Pelzel, Andrea Portanova, Erica Gelbard, and Carolyn Gill for believing in me and being so encouraging to help make this cookbook become a reality. The photography was made beautiful by an absolute dream team of Kristin Teig, photographer; Catrine Kelty and Karen Gillingham, food stylists; and their assistant Sam Hoppes; proving that sixty incredible photographs in five days really is possible! Thank you for making it happen in beautiful Charleston, South Carolina. My literary agents, Todd Shuster and Lori Galvin, you are forever stars in my eyes. Your guidance and kindness through this journey has kept me grounded and focused. Thank you. I can't wait to do it again.

Last but not least, I have to thank my husband, John, who does everything there is to do around the house (and yard), including emptying the dishwasher and making my coffee every single morning! To my children, who are my biggest cheerleaders and my biggest critics, and who keep me grounded: Adam, Shelby, and Sam, thank you for all of the fun, laughter, journeys, and tears (mostly mine) over the years. Here's to many, many more!

INDEX

ABOUT THE AUTHOR

KIM NELSON is the founder of Daisy Cakes, a South Carolina–based mail-order bakery that gained fans nationwide thanks to ABC's *Shark Tank*. Kim and Daisy Cakes have since been featured on ABC's *World News Now*, *The Queen Latifah Show*, *The Nate Berkus Show*, and Anderson Cooper's *Anderson Live*. Kim lives in Spartanburg, South Carolina, with her husband, John, their dog, Daisy, and a cat named Fuzzy.